CARPETS
AND FLOORING
FOR YOUR HOME

RENATE BEIGEL AND STANLEY LYONS

Quiller Press

First published 1995 by Quiller Press Limited,
46 Lillie Road, London SW6 1TN

ISBN 1 899163 09 3
© Stanley Lyons 1995
The authors hereby assert their moral right
to be identified as the authors of this book.

© Captions: Nicholas Hills 1995

Designed by Jo Lee
Produced by Hugh Tempest-Radford *Book Producers*
Colour reproduction by Yeo Valley Reproductions
Printed by Balding & Mansell

About the authors

Renate Beigel and Stanley Lyons, authors of *Lighting Your Home*, once again combine their talents to produce a book that all homemakers will value. Renate Beigel has had long experience of consumer products, and has tried to ensure that the information presented in this book is reader-friendly and potential-user-friendly. Stanley Lyons, an experienced technical author, provides a mass of information on all aspects of carpeting and flooring in a clear and concise way to help homemakers make wise economic choices when planning the flooring in their home.

Nicholas Hills, a practising architect and interior designer, wrote the captions and made a selection of the photographs.

Carpeting can provide an infinite variety of choice in anchoring a colour scheme for your room.

Contents

Authors' preface

Our aim is to help readers choose attractive, durable and economical carpeting, flooring or floorcoverings for their home.

Many homemakers have little knowledge about the qualities and attributes of the carpets and flooring products they see in the showroom. In addition to selecting products which will achieve harmony of style, colour and texture between the floor and the decor and other furnishings of a room (what we might call the 'pleasure aspect' of our floors), we should seek products that are durable and easy to maintain. With so much to choose from, and such wide variations in quality and price to juggle with, it seems sensible to arm ourselves with as much information as possible before we go out to buy.

The information in this book is presented in two parts:

Part 1 (Chapters 1 to 4) gives basic ideas about carpets, flooring and floorcoverings, describing the products, and providing you with the basis of making wise choices.

Part 2 (Chapters 5 to 8) gives guidelines on the preparation of floors before your carpets and other floorcoverings are laid, and then deals with their cleaning and care.

R.B. and S.L.
1995

Skilled weaving does not necessarily mean adherence to a rigid format. Here, the pattern of a modern Iranian Luri tribal rug from Robert Stevenson Carpets, has a geometric quality carried out with a relaxed sense of spacing. The hand dyed yarns also afford opportunities for subtle variations which bring the place vibrantly to life.

Creative minds can make the flooring for any room a beautiful feature. Overleaf a bathroom by Amtico.

Part 1

Basic ideas about Carpets, Flooring and Floorcoverings and how to choose wisely

Chapter 1

COLOUR, STYLE

and COMFORT *for your home*

How do the colours and textures of the surfaces of a room affect our perception of it?

Until we fill a room with our possessions and decorate its surfaces, it is just a neutral space waiting to be made into a comfortable human habitat. For example, wallpaper does much more than just cover up the plaster; it is an important factor in creating an ambiance in which we feel at home. If one had two rooms of identical size in which the walls were decorated differently, one room might take on a cold clinical appearance, while the other could adopt the feeling of comfort, familiarity and relaxation.

The coverings of the walls and floor largely determine the character of a room; indeed, if you were to enter a room which was decorated and carpeted but otherwise completely empty, you would know at once if it was intended to be a living room, a bedroom or a playroom. The area of the floor is typically nearly a fifth of the total surface area of a room, and the colour and texture of the floor surface can have even greater visual impact on the occupants of a room than does the wallpaper. Carpets and floor coverings not only provide colour and pattern, but are the surface upon which we walk and thus make contact with the structure of the room. If you are creating a new home and starting with empty undecorated rooms, you will have the freedom to adopt any basic colour scheme, and to seek curtains, carpets and furnishings either to match or to contrast. This gives scope for individual choice by the homemaker, depending on their personality, age and lifestyle.

Whatever your taste, the precision of a neat floorcovering provides a civilising background for the rest of the room. Decorwool carpet from Wools of New Zealand.

How important is the floor in the creation of a pleasing interior?

The floor sets the tone of the whole of any inhabited space. It can provide the basis

3

Carpets for an elegant living room can be plain, patterned or have the pattern formed by sculpting the surface. In the first example (left), the Palace Velvet carpet by Brintons has an inlaid border of an analogous plain colour to define the sitting area. The charming small scaled pattern of the Axminster weave carpet by Ulster Carpet Mills (below) provides a focus for a small room and makes a light colour, which is useful for reflecting daylight into the room, more practical in disguising the odd mark or two.

The skillfully sculpted carpet, designed by architect Nicholas Hills, is made by Stockwell Carpets. Here (below right), a one colour carpet is given interest and form by being sculpted in the finishing process to form a trellis design.

for the whole decor of the room. If the flooring is unsuitable for the functions of the room, you may have a room in which you never feel quite comfortable.

Not only does the flooring play an important role in the creation of the style and ambiance of an interior, but, by your choice of carpet, textile floor covering or hard flooring, you largely determine the character of the room – by its physical qualities as well as by its colour. Therefore, in setting about creating an interior of any kind, the choice of type of flooring should be your first decision. If it is not possible for you to harmonise the decor of the room with the nature and colour of the flooring, nothing you do will prevent it from spoiling the effect that you are striving for.

Are there any 'golden rules' about colour and decor which simply must not be broken?

No. Choosing colour and decor is an activity in which you have great freedom to express yourself. The quiet, play-it-safe character will probably want everything to harmonise, and may choose 'safe' neutral colours, while someone of a more outgoing personality may want their home to make a statement about themselves and to define their role in society. All this can be signified by the colours and patterns that we select for our homes.

How may one set about planning the colour scheme for a room?

If you are refurbishing a room which already has satisfactory decor, or if you are about to purchase a new carpet to harmonise with the colours of your existing curtains and upholstery, you will be constrained in your choice of carpet and flooring colours by the colours already in use. You might, for example, choose a carpet which matches the dominant colour in the room, or one which will harmonise pleasantly with the colours of existing curtains and furnishings.

In some situations you might allow your colour scheme to be led by a single dominant factor, such as the colour of the upholstery of an existing suite of furniture, or that of a visually dominant fireplace, or the colour of some beautiful natural wood or veneered doors.

If the room already has curtains which you wish to retain, and it is intended to allow their colour to be one of the visual themes of the room, it is easy enough to change the colours of your existing upholstered furniture with loose covers.

Remember that an unwise decision about the colours of your carpet or floor covering could be the most expensive mistake you ever make in the process of homemaking! You should, therefore, give considerable thought to this important matter. Well-chosen carpeting or flooring, in harmony with tasteful decor and appropriate furnishings, can promote feelings of warmth and relaxation, and impart an atmosphere of comfort – or even luxury – to your room.

What effect does a dominant colour have in the decor of a room?

When we enter a room which has large areas of one strong colour, a process of **colour adaptation** takes place, the degree of adaptation varying with the period of exposure. Most of this adaptation takes place within a few minutes; complete adaptation can take upwards of an hour.

The effect of colour adaptation can be demonstrated by putting on a pair of spectacles with coloured lenses. For example, if we put on pink-tinted glasses, at first everything we see appears to be tinged with pink, but after a few minutes the pink appearance of our surroundings seems to fade away and colours are again normal. However, if, when the adaptation is well advanced, the pink-tinted glasses are removed, one gets the illusion that everything is tinged with **green**, i.e. the complementary colour to pink. Then again, the process of adaptation takes place, and after a while the sensation of greenness wears off.

A similar thing occurs when we enter a room which has large areas of a single strong colour. For example, consider what would be the effect in a room decorated mainly in strong yellows. The light entering the room from the windows or coming from the electric lighting, being reflected from the room surfaces, would take on a yellow tinge. When you entered the room, red objects in the room would tend to look orange, and blue objects would tend to look greenish – you would be struck by the overall yellow appearance of the whole room. However, after a short time, as your eyes became adapted to the dominant colour, the scene would soon appear to be perfectly normal, the sense of yellowness decreasing and the distortion of other colours fading away until they seemed to be as they always were – in other words, your eyes would have become adapted to the dominant colour. Your state of colour-adaptation would be demonstrated if, while still yellow-adapted, you went immediately into another room, where you might be astonished to find that your favourite blue vase had apparently turned green, and your familiar red curtains were now orange! However, once you were away from the yellow environment, your eyes would rapidly re-adjust, and all the colours around you would look normal again.

From the above, you will see that one must exercise great care when planning to use a single dominant colour in any room for its decor, furnishings and carpets.

Some successful room decoration is achieved by using varying tones and shades of one colour. It can be just as difficult to get the balance right as it is in using several colours together, but a room like this using Brinton's Majestic carpet with an inlaid border, might be just the thing for a south-facing bedroom, providing the illusion of space and the impression of coolness.

What effect does the lighting have on the appearance of a room?

The appearance of the colours in your carpet or other flooring, and the other furnishings, depends upon the nature of the light that illuminates them. The colour appearance of a lamp is no guide to its colour rendering, i.e. the ability of the light from a lamp to render non-white colours faithfully. The familiar 'warm coloured' lighting from filament lamps is deficient in blue (as compared with daylight) and thus actually renders colours rather poorly. However, the somewhat 'cooler coloured' light from modern fluorescent lamps generally renders colours rather better.

The colour properties of daylight vary all the time, so you should never judge colours by the shop lighting alone; and do not place too much reliance on taking colour samples to the door of the shop to look at them either! Colours are easier to judge when there is plenty of light, but they still might look quite different under electric lighting. Of course, you want your carpets, floor coverings and other furnishings to look good under both daylight and electric lighting conditions.

The lighting in your home is probably achieved at present mainly by the use of ordinary filament lamps; however, even if you do not already use the new highly economical energy-saving **compact fluorescent lamps**, it is very likely that you will use them in the future. Therefore you would be wise to examine colour samples under the light both from filament lamps and compact fluorescent lamps. If this is not done, you could be disappointed with the colour-appearance of your new carpet after it is installed. (Compact fluorescent lamps and many other lighting matters are explained simply in the authors' book *Lighting Your Home*.)

Remember the effect that strongly coloured decor can have on colours as they are perceived. In any room, light that is reflected from a coloured surface is changed by selective reflection and absorption of the various colours of which the light is composed, so it takes on a composition determined at least in part by the colours in the room. So, if you are going to use a strongly coloured wallpaper, put a sample patch of the proposed carpet or floor covering against a sample patch of the paper, and see what effect reflected light from each has on the other.

Here (right), Brintons Palace Portico design continues the colour used in the bookcases, but provides a telling contrast with the rich quality of polished timber and leather-bound books. A sense of mystery is created by the sharp contrast between the pools of light and the shaded areas.

An altogether different effect is achieved by bouncing light off a Raspberry pink Sanderson carpet, where a classic contrast is made between shades of pink and fresh, light green.

As explained above, the light reflected from the surfaces of a room will take on a tinge of the dominant colour. Therefore, you will be less likely to make mistakes if you use only pale colours for your general decor, such as white, cream, very pale eau-de-nil, very pale greys or magnolia. These will not greatly change the colour of light reflected from them, and thus your choice of colours will be achieved whether viewed in daylight or under electric lighting.

Remember also that the floor will reflect light. Light from downlighters will be reflected from the floor, so that the ceiling and walls will take on a pale tint of the dominant colour of your carpet or floor covering. This effect can be quite noticeable if you have white or very pale-coloured ceiling and walls.

The stunning effect achieved by using a plain natural coloured Wilton Royal carpet in a living room largely composed of similar pale colours. Rooms like this are best kept for adult use and the surfaces and textiles kept scrupulously cleaned – otherwise the effect is ruined.

Can the use of different flooring materials in adjacent rooms be successful?

There is no reason for all the rooms to have the same floor treatment. The appearance of floors may vary very greatly with the materials used – vinyl, cork, ceramic tiles, wood, carpet, rugs etc – but their colours can create harmony between the different materials. Contrasts of colour and texture between adjacent areas can be most attractive. For example, one might stand in an entrance hall which has a timber-effect or parquet floor, and peek into the kitchen which has a vinyl or cork-tile floor or a ceramic tiled floor; looking into the living room one might see a patterned carpet, and perhaps there would be a plain carpet on the stairway. For the floor of the bathroom or shower room, you might use ceramic tiles or a water-resistant type of carpet. Ceramic tiles or quarry tiles would be suitable in a conservatory or glazed patio, their colour and texture contrasting pleasantly with that of the carpet in the adjacent living room.

In all the rooms of your home you can make tasteful use of rugs and mats in harmonising or contrasting colours to the flooring or carpeting. The important thing is to select flooring of a character and colour appropriate to each area, and to give expression to your personal taste as the creative homemaker.

An easy way to vary the decor is to have a richly designed rug which can easily be put down in the centre of the room, such as this one by Stockwell Carpets.

Chapter 2

TYPES *of carpets*

and their PROPERTIES

On a cold day, why does a carpeted room feel warmer than a room with a hard floor?

There may be a psychological factor to this feeling because we tend to associate carpets with warmth and comfort, but it is also a fact that a carpet provides a measure of **thermal insulation**, i.e. it reduces the amount of heat-loss through the floor. This makes the room cheaper to heat, as well as tending to keep the room at a more even temperature.

An attribute of carpets that is sometimes overlooked is their contribution to the **humidity balance** of a room, an effect most marked in the case of carpets with a high wool content. This is explained as follows. If your room had impervious walls and other surfaces, in cold damp weather and in unheated conditions every surface would be running with condensation like a chilly dungeon. But the plastering and paper of the walls and ceilings in modern homes tends to absorb excess atmospheric humidity so that the room feels dry and warm. Next time we air the room, the moisture held in the absorbent room surfaces is released, so that our home remains dry and comfortable. Damp air, being colder and heavier, tends to descend towards the floor; it will be apparent that adding the absorbent qualities of a large area of carpet will improve the humidity balance, and hence make the room feel warmer.

There is nothing to match the feeling of luxury provided by a good carpet well laid on a good underlay. The Chinese Water Dragon design by Firth Carpets has in addition an appealing all-over pattern of oriental richness. In fitting to a room thought might be given to providing it with a plain border so as to calm the effect down at the junction with walls and curtains.

What are the acoustic effects of carpeting a room?

Carpeting provides a measure of **noise insulation**, reducing the amount of sound entering or leaving the room through the floor, thus making the room more private, softening footsteps, and reducing the noise nuisance between rooms.

Another important result of carpeting a room is the **acoustic dampening effect**.

You will notice that as soon as your new carpet is laid, it kills the echo. In an empty, uncarpeted room, the 'period of reverberation' of sound (as it bounces about from wall to wall) is much longer than that in a room full of people. The softness of the carpet absorbs this echo, making the room feel comfortably 'occupied'.

The acoustic dampening effect is of considerable importance, as was made clear in a discussion the authors had with an elderly lady who had recently taken possession of a flat having concrete floors which were covered with vinyl. She had just had the flat carpeted throughout and told us, "When I first arrived here, I thought I had made a mistake in buying this flat. It always seemed chilly, and somehow empty, even though I had my furniture and curtains in place. Hearing my own footsteps as I moved about made me feel very much alone. But, as soon as the new carpeting was laid, the whole place somehow **sounded** more comfortable, as well as feeling much warmer."

Is the texture of the carpet important?

Yes, of great importance. To most people, to speak of 'a comfortable room' immediately conjures up an image of a room with a beautiful and luxurious carpet. It is often the appreciation of the 'give' and 'bounce' of the carpet underfoot that imparts that feeling of comfort.

A pleasant texture, softness, and a feeling of warmth to the touch – these are factors you will appreciate every time you enter your room, even though you usually have contact with the carpet only through the soles of your shoes. However, if, when relaxing in your chair before the fire or tv, you should kick off your shoes, your stockinged feet will tell you that you were right to choose a carpet with a texture that you like.

Not only colour, but texture has a telling effect in surface quality and reflection of light. Natural, heathery shades work very well when you have no intention of either trying to match armchair covers or of changing what you already have in a room – as in these examples from Brinton Carpets.

You don't have to live in a large country house like Chatsworth (left) to enjoy the effect of a cleverly bordered carpet. Almost any regular space can make use of a border design to give form and emphasis to the floor surface as, for example, with the Brintons Majestic design. Borders are also particularly useful for a staircase in filling the space to each side of a narrow width weave, enabling the treads to be fully carpeted (right).

(Overleaf) A really classy border will lift a plain carpet into a different world. Stockwell Carpets will make any design up for you in colours of your choice.

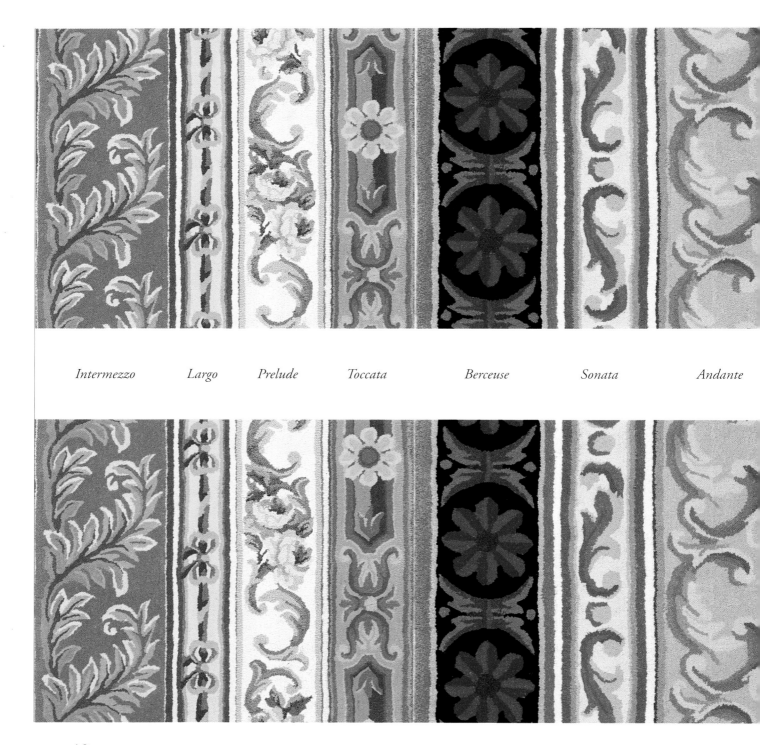

Intermezzo   *Largo*   *Prelude*   *Toccata*   *Berceuse*   *Sonata*   *Andante*

Impromptu   *Ballade*   *Allegro*   *Nocturne*   *Fugue*   *Scherzo*   *Fantasia*

How does the material of which a carpet is made affect its quality and properties?

In Chapter 1 we discussed colour and design; important though these are, there are other factors which should be considered, and which would be difficult to rank in order of importance.

We should be concerned with choosing a carpet that will give us satisfaction in terms of its softness and bounce; we should certainly attempt to find a carpet which will give us durable wear over a long period. Certainly, most buyers will be concerned with the price. If we combine these three factors, we arrive at the important objective of **value for money**.

The pile material determines most of the characteristics of a carpet. In the past, many types of materials have been used as the pile in carpets; most modern carpets have a pile consisting of pure wool, or of a synthetic fibre (e.g. nylon or polypropylene), or a mixture of wool and synthetic fibre. The key facts are as follows:

◆ **All-wool carpets.** There is no doubt that a good-quality all-wool carpet is delightful. Properly maintained and treated reasonably kindly, it will certainly keep its good looks better than many cheaper types of carpet made from synthetic materials. All-wool carpets compact less, keep their looks for longer and have good resistance to scorching by a dropped cigarette end. Some major British carpet manufacturers make nothing but carpets with a 100% wool content.

◆ **Synthetic fibre carpets.** Some, but not all, of the ranges of cheaper carpets are made of 100% synthetic fibre. If well made, and well cared for, they will probably outlast all other kinds of carpets, but will not necessarily look as well in your room. If it is necessary to wet-clean them, synthetic-fibre carpets may be less prone to damage from wetting than are all-wool or wool-mixture carpets. Such carpets may have a 'built-in' stain-resistant treatment which can help to keep them clean.

◆ **Wool/synthetic fibre mixture carpets.** These are designed to combine the benefits of the comfort of wool with the durability and strength of a synthetic fibre. It is claimed, and research has shown, that the synthetic-fibre content helps to

In small spaces it really tells to have one carpet laid throughout. Here, Brintons Bell twist in 80:20 mix, effortlessly unites hall and living room.

resist wear by abrasion of the pile material. This quality of abrasion resistance should be borne in mind when buying stair carpet. Some major British carpet manufacturers make nothing but carpets with a content of 80% wool and 20% nylon. Such blends of fibres are used to gain the benefits of the attributes of both materials; for example, blends of wool and nylon combine the maximum natural softness and spring of wool with increased resistance to wear and soiling resulting from the inclusion of man-made fibre.

What is the significance of the 'British Wool' symbol?

This symbol may be displayed in advertisements and carpet manufacturers' literature, as well as on the labels on carpets. It signifies that the product has either a 100% wool pile, or an 80%/20% wool/nylon mixture where at least 80% of the total fibre content is wool, and at least 50% of the wool has been grown in the UK.

What is the significance of the 'Decorwool' trademark?

'Decorwool' is the brandname of Wools of New Zealand, and is applied only to wool carpets which meet very high standards. Some twenty different performance tests are carried out on Decorwool-branded carpets, and these must be met before they can carry this Wools of New Zealand brand mark. A number of British carpet manufacturers make Decorwool branded carpets; for example, the 'Madrigal' range of stain-resistant and crush-resistant carpets from Cavalier Carpets which contain 80% wool, 10% nylon and 10% polyester.

Can carpets containing synthetic fibres generate static electricity?

Yes, and so may pure woollen carpets too in dry atmospheric conditions. The electric charge is caused by the friction of normal use. In certain very dry conditions, this can result in actual sparks both being seen and heard – and felt when electrically charged metal objects are touched. The effect is quite harmless and does not generate any heat. If the carpet acquires an electrostatic charge, it will tend to attract dust particles, and thus will be more difficult to keep clean.

The tendency for a carpet to generate static electricity may be dealt with by the application of an anti-static treatment during manufacture, though this may tend to become ineffective over a period of time or if the carpet is wet-cleaned. Some carpet backings are made electrically conductive to leak away any electrostatic charge.

Anti-static aerosol sprays are available for home use, but these should be used with care. As the vapour may be flammable, do not smoke, expose a flame, nor use any electrical appliance while the vapour may be present. Treat a small out-of-sight test area before using the treatment generally. Remember that some people are sensitive to such sprays, so keep the windows open during spraying and for a period afterwards until the room is thoroughly aired.

In most cases, all that may be necessary in very dry atmospheres is to increase the room humidity level slightly. This can be done using humidifiers, the simplest form of which just clip on to the radiators. Even keeping houseplants in the room can help!

What is a shag pile carpet?

A shag pile carpet is a tufted carpet having a pile greater than 15mm in height, but the pile is not dense. Such carpets have a decidedly luxurious look and feel about them, and are certainly very comfortable underfoot, but have gone out of fashion because they require special care, including occasional raking (with a special rake that your carpet retailer can supply) to bring up the flattened pile. Also be aware of possible danger to small babies from shag pile carpets, especially those of poor quality, for hairy bits might be pulled out by a baby who could choke on them.

Are all kinds of carpets equally good at resisting stains?

No. Generally, carpets made from synthetic fibre (e.g. nylon, polypropylene etc) will be more stain-resistant than pure wool or wool-mixture carpets. Wool pile and wool mixture carpets are more resistant to cigarette burns than are carpets having their pile made entirely from synthetic fibre.

For a busily occupied family room, you will be looking for a carpet with good resistance to the staining which may occur due to spillages and 'accidents' by small children or pets.

Special treatments of synthetic fibre piles, such as the 'Stainmaster' treatment from Du Pont, are intended to make the carpet more resistant to staining and soiling. Anti-staining treatment may be applied to the fibres from which the carpet is made, or the treatment may be applied to the manufactured carpet. (In Chapter 7 ways of cleaning soiled carpets and removing stains are discussed.)

What is meant by the 'construction' of a carpet?

The term 'construction' is used to describe not only the method by which the carpet has been made, but also the materials used and the way they have been used, e.g. the pile weight and the pile thickness or pile density. The basic methods of pile carpet constructions are: **woven** carpets (e.g. Axminster and Wilton), **tufted** carpets, and **fusion bonded** carpets. Other types of textile floorcoverings are fibre bonded carpets and flocked carpets.

All UK woven carpet is made either by the Axminster or the Wilton method. Although the materials used in Axminster and Wilton carpets are the same, the weaving methods are quite different.

What are the characteristics of Axminster carpet?

In making Axminster carpet, the pile is inserted one row of tufts at a time, each row representing a section of the overall pattern. The tufts are 'U'-shaped, and are anchored at the bottom into the primary backing which is woven at the same time. The backing may have a synthetic-starch or latex finish applied to it.

Because the weaving method permits a wide range of colours to be used, Axminster weaving has been traditionally used mostly for creating multicoloured patterned carpets; however, styles have changed, and many modern Axminster carpets do not have the large ornate designs with which this type of carpet was formerly associated.

WOVEN

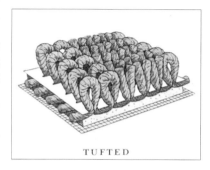

TUFTED

The contrast in construction between woven and tufted carpets is best explained by means of diagrams.

23

What are the characteristics of Wilton carpet?

The Wilton weaving method is used largely for creating plain carpet and patterned carpet with up to five colours. In this type of weaving, the pile and the backing materials are closely interwoven. In patterned Wiltons, the pile yarn not appearing on the surface is woven into the backing, thus producing a very firm and dimensionally stable material.

Variations in the traditional Wilton weaving method include 'carved pile' carpets and a type of loop-pile carpet too. Some Wilton carpets are manufactured by what is known as the 'face-to-face' method or 'sandwich weaving' in which two carpets are woven simultaneously, and then the pile strands in the 'sandwich' are slit apart to form two lengths of carpet.

(Right) Small areas of rooms can be emphasised by inlaying a contrasting colour possibly with a border to surround it. Such inlays best relate to the proportion of a room and a particular feature, such as a window or fireplace. If you did need to take up an area usually carpeted, say for dancing, or even playing with the toy train, this would be the way to do it, securing the edges with Velcro tape. (Brintons Majestic.)

What are the characteristics of tufted carpet?

The pile materials used in manufacturing tufted carpet are basically the same as those used in woven carpets, but the form of construction is different. Tufted carpet is made by inserting the pile material with needles into a **primary backing**. The complex machine that is used somewhat resembles a multi-needle sewing machine. The primary backings are usually made from a synthetic pre-woven material or a non-woven material. The pile material is anchored into the primary backing by an adhesive (usually a latex compound). A secondary backing is then added to the carpet to complete its manufacture.

(Left) More classically designed rooms can still have fitted carpet, even though it was more usual in the past to have loose laid carpets with a timber surround. This Brintons Serenade design works well with the border cut into it, especially if it follows the profile of a room.

What are the characteristics of fusion-bonded carpet?

In this type of carpet, the pile adheres to the backing very firmly, making tuft loss practically impossible, and fraying at cut edges very unlikely. The carpet is not patterned, and the pile has a soft velvet appearance. Because of the method of manufacture, the backing is less flexible than in other types of pile carpets, giving excellent dimensional stability. There can be problems in using such a stiff carpet for stairs.

What are the characteristics of fibre-bonded carpet?

Fibre-bonded carpet is made by 'needling' a web of synthetic fibres to form a felted surface. This is finished with a backing of pvc or bituminous material to give dimensional stability. Other types of fibre bonded carpet may have a raised surface of fibres or a nap. This type of floorcovering is hard-wearing; it is used mostly in commercial locations, though DIY stores cater to the market for easy-to-lay floor tiles in this material.

Striking geometric designs, such as this Hadschlu rug from the Marco Polo range by Louis de Poortere, capture the ancient richness of carpet design which have made them so highly valued for centuries. Much pleasure can be had from contemplating the pattern as one's eyes move from one part to the other as it does in gazing at the moving flames of a fire.

What are the characteristics of a Berber carpet?

The term 'Berber' (or 'Berber style') originally referred to hand-woven rugs made in North Africa from undyed woollen yarn. It now describes carpets made from natural coloured wool or from dyed yarn having a 'natural' appearance. Maybe termed a 'heather' weave.

Is there ever a sound case for buying the very cheapest carpets?

Clearly some people think so, but it is doubtful if one really gets good value for money from some of the cheaper products. On the other hand, it must be admitted that some people consider they get good value by buying very cheap carpets which have poor wearing quality or resistance to staining etc, and replacing them quite frequently.

One should take note of the new developments in carpets. For example, if you want to carpet a kitchen floor which gets lots of spillage and mess, you could consider buying a type of carpet termed 'kitchen carpet'.

The carpet trade use the term 'Berber' to denote carpets made from natural colour wool or from yarn which is dyed but retaining its irregularly spun characteristics. Here, heather blue Berber can take a punishing wear on both steps and floor surface. (Brintons.)

What are the characteristics of 'kitchen carpet'?

These are fusion-bonded 'flocked' carpets with a high-density short pile of synthetic fibre, made in a single colour or with a printed pattern. They have very little bounce, but are water-resistant, easy to clean, and very durable. (For example, Flotex kitchen carpet has a 10-year guarantee against wear.)

This type of flocked carpet has a very low pile or nap formed of short lengths of polyamide fibre which, in manufacture, are electrostatically attracted (or 'shot') into a waterproof adhesive-treated backing. Because of their very dense short pile, such carpets are easy to clean and are highly moisture-resistant. They are a very practical solution to the problem of carpeting kitchens and bathrooms.

Would 'kitchen carpet' be suitable for a bathroom?

Kitchen carpet as described in the previous answer would be satisfactory in a bathroom provided the bathroom is not subject to a great deal of wetting or condensation. (Condensation will be minimised by having suitable heating and by ventilating the bathroom when it is not in use.)

Problems may arise if water gets under the edge of the carpet, for this could cause mould to grow, or could encourage damp rot in a wooden floor. However, if the carpet was well fixed down at the edges with a water-resistant adhesive as recommended by the carpet manufacturer, it probably would be satisfactory. For a bathroom in which there is likely to be considerable wetting, a suitably installed tiled floor might be more suitable – as discussed in Chapter 3.

Can I be certain that lengths of carpet of different widths, made by the same manufacturer and purchased at the same time, will be a good colour match?

Not necessarily. The label on the carpet will tell you if carpet of different widths from the same batch are or are not guaranteed to match. For example, the label might state that carpet of 2m and 4m widths from the same batch will be a good colour match, but that carpet of 4.57m width is not guaranteed to colour-match with carpet of other widths. In general manufacturers cannot guarantee that carpet dyed to the same colour specification but from different batches will be perfectly matched.

An ideal soft floor covering in a kitchen/living room is provided by the Bonar and Flotex short pile synthetic fibre surface with a waterproof adhesive treated backing. Children love it, but it must be kept immaculately clean so germs and microbes don't enjoy it too.

What is the importance of the backing of a carpet?

While some kinds of rugs have a pattern that goes all the way through (some are reversible), woven, tufted and bonded carpets are always one-sided. In all carpet constructions, the 'use surface', that is, the fibre tufts, are anchored into the backing which gives the carpet dimensional stability. Non-woven carpets usually have a primary backing to which the tufts are attached. To give an improved feel underfoot and improved dimensional stability, these carpets usually also have a **secondary backing** made of woven jute, or of synthetic material, or foam. In some cases pvc or solid latex are used instead. The secondary backing to a carpet greatly improves the 'body' of the finished product and enhances its handling properties.

A carpet gives valuable insulation against heat loss through the floor. The provision of a substantial backing enhances this insulation effect, as well as protecting the carpet to some extent from wear due to unevenness in the floor under it.

Carpets provide a high degree of sound insulation through the floor, a quality particularly valuable in the case of upstairs rooms which have boarded floors. In Chapter 5 we discuss the preparation of floors to receive carpeting, including the laying of underfloors and underlays to provide a level surface for the carpet and to enhance the thermal and acoustic insulation.

Why is there such a big difference in price between the cheapest and most expensive carpets?

The price difference arises because of differences in quality, including such factors as:

◆ whether the carpet is of woven, tufted or fusion-bonded construction etc;

◆ the fibre material of which the pile is made (wool, synthetic fibre, or a mixture of both);

◆ the density of the pile (the number of tufts per square inch or per square millimetre);

◆ the length of the pile above the backing;

◆ the finished weight of the pile (in grammes per square metre or ounces per square yard);

◆ the number of colours woven in, the nature of the pattern, and the degree of colourfastness;

◆ treatments applied to the fibre, to the backing or to the finished carpet to improve attributes such as: fire resistance, staining resistance, freedom from static electricity;

◆ the quality and thickness of the primary and secondary backing.

As when buying any other product, you only get what you pay for!

What are the special features of the most expensive carpets?

As well as having the special degree of softness and bounce that you would expect, the quality features may include elegant patterns and the availability of matching borders to the body carpet. Some top range carpets are available with motifs or ruglike insets woven into the main area of the carpet.

What are the virtues of carpet tiles?

Carpet tiles have the virtue that stained or damaged tiles can be taken up and replaced. Also, a tiled carpet enables easy access to underfloor services if necessary.

A chance to 'do it yourself' with Heuga carpet tiles. If you want clear bright colours you can slice the yellow and green tiles diagonally and compose them into a zig-zag patterned border, as in this child's bedroom, using Heuga's Accord range

Carpet tiles are available in several sizes, usually 400mm (16 inches) square or 500mm (20 inches) square. They come in various constructions including tufted carpet, flocked carpet, needlefelt etc. One type, which is very successful, is of a felt construction containing a proportion of animal fibre (sheep or goat's wool). Some carpet tiles have an adhesive backing, but some are simply laid loose, or held in place with double-sided adhesive tape. The most common method of fitting carpet tiles is to use a release adhesive.

When carefully laid on a smooth floor, the edges of the tiles tend to amalgamate so that the joins are not noticeable. To give the impression of a continuous carpet, the pile of all the tiles must be laid in the same direction; however, by turning alternate tiles, a chequered appearance is created. Carpet tiles of two colours can be laid to give a chequered appearance. Other designs can be devised, including borders of a different colour to the body of the carpet.

31

Striking contrasts can be obtained with the same technique, here composed
into a diamond to define a seating area with Heuga's Bistro range.

Might our choice of carpeting be affected by the fact that we have a cat or a dog?

Tufted carpets are more likely to be damaged by animal claws than other types of carpets, and certainly a shag pile carpet would not be a good choice if you have domestic pets. In general you would be well advised to have short-pile woven or flocked carpet, and you might wish to consider having woven 100% synthetic fibre carpet. Flocked 'kitchen carpet' with a water resistant back seems almost immune to damage by pets.

What are the uses of rugs and mats?

Waveney Applegrowers make a rush matting, medieval in its simplicity and style. Whilst it looks wonderful, it does not like sharp heels and abrasive wear. Used before a fire it might be treated with a fire retardant as, unlike a wool rug, it is not naturally flame resisting.

In carpeted rooms, at places where a great deal of wear is likely to take place, such as in front of the sofa and armchairs and in front of the fireplace, a rug can be both practical and decorative. In the winter months, when soiling is most likely, additional rugs may be put down in the hallway and other places where there is a lot of foot traffic.

Elderly people who sit for long hours find that their feet keep warmer if they have a rug in front of their favourite armchair, especially in rooms which have a solid floor,

and particularly if there is not a thick insulating underlay under the carpet.

It was formerly a common practice to place a small mat, termed a **slip mat**, in hallways outside each door. Modern mats can be obtained with a rubberised backing which prevents slipping on smooth flooring and prevents them from 'walking' if they are laid on a carpet.

In Chapter 6 we discuss the value of doormats to prevent dust and dirt being walked into the house. If new flooring is to be laid in a hall or room with an external door, consider getting your builder to create a 'mat well', i.e. a floor recess to receive the doormat. The recess should be slightly bigger than the doormat and deep enough to bring the top of the doormat level with the flooring.

In rooms having some form of hard flooring (vinyl, cork, linoleum etc), rugs can provide a pleasant softening effect and can bring some very welcome colour to an otherwise rather plain room.

(Left) A magnificent Quashgai Gabbeh rug, here used to fill the centre of a sitting room. (Fired Earth.)

Stockwell Carpets will make you a 2.44 metres square rug in a needlepoint loop with a velvet pile border, such as the Millefiore design shown here from their Botanical Collection designed by Robert Holmes. They will match to special colours or indeed make a whole carpet to fit the exact profile of a room.

Are there any other uses of rugs for decoration?

A form of room decor that is popular in the Middle East and Far East is to use rugs and carpets as wall decorations. In modern European homes, this seems to work well if the size of the rug is not too overpowering for the size of the room. A colourful Indian rug, perhaps highlighted with one or two spotlights or a 'picture light', could be a most striking and colourful feature of your decor. To display a rug on a wall, the rug should be attached to a bar or rod at its top edge, and the bar suspended on supports fixed firmly to the wall.

(Above) Wall hanging rug by Beverley Needlepoint.

It was a custom in Victorian times to protect a grand piano by spreading a beautifully embroidered shawl or a small rug across its top; rugs would also be used to cover other large items of furniture, with a vase of flowers or other ornament placed upon it. Small colourful rugs, lightweight enough to be flexible, are sometimes laid on the back of a sofa for decorative effect. You could use these ideas if they are compatible with the style of your decor.

What types of decorative rugs and mats are available?

The choice is so great that, to describe all the styles and weaves would fill a book! We can only mention some of the popular types and advise that the range of prices is very wide, from a few pounds for the cheapest, up to thousands of pounds for beautifully crafted handmade rugs imported from the Middle East, the Far East, or the Indian subcontinent. An interesting book to refer to is *Oriental Carpets* by Charles Ellis (see Appendix 1 – References). An excellent write-up on tribal rugs (and on many types of tiling too) is given in the publication *Applying Arts* available from Fired Earth. An interesting catalogue of imported rugs made of natural materials is available from Crucial Trading Ltd.

Rugs come in many dimensions and proportions, there being no standardised sizes. Those which are narrow and long (say, under a metre wide and 2m or more longer) are referred to as 'runners' and are particularly useful in hallways and passages.

(Left) The ruby wine reds of this Quashgai rug are peculiarly appropriate to the dining room where a feeling of well-being is induced by the rich colours. (Fired Earth.)

(Above right) Crisp and classic designs are provided in natural fibre mats by Threshold Floorings of Swindon. They are ideal for laying over a tiled floor when a softer effect is required.

Axminster Rya rugs – Usually British made, unpatterned, with a longish pile which may tend to flatten. The true Rya is a Scandinavian carpet, a work of art, more often found on the wall

Coir matting – Coir fibre is used to make slightly hairy but very hardy runners that you can put down anywhere. They may be used in passages or laid on any type of hard flooring. Coir runners come typically in two sizes, 700mm x 7m (28in x 23ft) and 1m x 10m (33in x 33ft). They can be cut into shorter lengths if required. It is not too difficult to bind the ends or to sew shorter lengths together. Coir is also used to make very reasonably priced boucle bleached rugs in pale straw colours, and may have a coloured or black stitched border. Coir mats with strong two-colour patterns are also available.

Annette Nix is a designer with a spectacular vision of what carpets can be when released from a conventional straightjacket. Here (left), her modern design for a period panelled room shows how thrilling the combination of new and old can be.

(Below) Traditional Scotch carpet has its modern variations in these Oban rugs from Threshold Floorings. The beauty is that when they get dirty they can be popped into the washing machine, so they are ideal for slip mats or to protect the main carpet in vulnerable areas, near a wash basin or dressing table perhaps, or to stop the 'tread' from a stone floor marking an adjoining carpet.

Cotton rugs – Imports of these from Third World countries are usually unbranded. Some are woven in a range of colours, some are printed. They may not be colour fast for washing but can possibly be dry-cleaned.

Durrie – A mat woven from sorghum grass.

Handwoven rugs – Created by individual British craftsmen in a wide range of types and patterns. May be quite expensive. Some are delightfully colourful.

Hessian – Loose hessian mats are not usually very successful unless provided with a stiff backing. Wall-to-wall hessian can be an economical way of covering a floor on which there is little foot traffic, especially if rugs or mats are placed at the areas of greatest wear. The hessian must be secured at the edges to hold it taut, and must be well protected by a wooden or metal nosing at the door threshold.

Indian rugs – So called, but they may be tribal rugs from countries other than India – especially the Middle East. These rugs are woven on hand-looms with the pile looped and knotted into the backing. Those of good quality may give reasonable wear, but cheaper ones are likely to flatten soon in use and may lose a lot of their body by fluffing. Such rugs made by nomadic tribesmen may be made of any kind of animal hair and are distinguished by their unique patterns.

Jute – Jute rugs are soft underfoot and so are suitable to lay over hard floors in bedrooms. Their natural appearance goes well with wooden flooring. Jute rugs come in simple herringbone weave in a limited range of plain colours with fringed ends. Typical sizes are: 1m x 1.5m (39in x 5ft); 1.4m x 2m (54in x 6ft 6in), and 1.6m x 2.3m (5ft 3in x 7ft 6in). Jute is also used to weave attractive herringbone patterned runners with sewn borders in contrasting colours.

Kilims – (or kelims) The term describes traditional oriental tapestry-woven rugs or other textile pieces, as well as attractive modern rugs made in boucle bleached coir. The latter are available with complex patterns, some being decorated with letters, numbers and illustrations of animals for nursery use.

Natural fibre matting – Matting made of natural materials such as seagrass, rushes or sisal may not stand up to heavy traffic but can provide an economical flooring treatment for an adult bedroom or a room where the main foot traffic is over rugs placed on the rush matting. Wall-to-wall matting of this kind may tend to 'walk', and may ruck up near furniture legs. Some better quality machine-woven rugs and mats of British manufacture are made of jute and reinforced with a small percentage of synthetic fibre to produce a more dimensionally stable product.

Numdah rugs – Indian rugs in which the pattern is embroidered on to a felt base. Some are very colourful. They are cheap, but unlikely to be very durable.

Seagrass squares – These are a tough basic form of economical matting, the small squares typically being sewn together to form mats of 1.2m x 1.8m (4ft x 7ft). They can be simply put down and pushed together to cover larger areas. Pleasant in feel and texture, they can give long life. Seagrass is similar to sisal in its general qualities but rather coarser.

Sisal – This natural fibre is used to weave two types of rugs 'linen' style (single colour) and 'plaid' woven which may have a woven plain or patterned border in contrasting colours.

Wool – (of sheep or goats) is used to create unpatterned flatweave rugs, usually with a linen border in a contrasting colour. Some rugs are embellished with a leather border, or with a decorative tapestry border.

Tapestry – Handmade carpets, made in Madeira or Portugal.

In the types of rugs described above which are hand woven by individual craftsmen, there may be variations in colour or dimensions between similar rugs. Some hints on rugs that curl or slip are given in Chapter 8.

Owning an original Savonnerie carpet is not given to many today but Stockwell Carpets have recreated the spirit of the period in their Tribute collection. The illustration shows their Napoleon design, 3.00 x 4.50 metres.

The diligence of Madeiran needlewomen is renowned and the beauty of their stitchwork is second to none. In this rug half cross stitch has been used to create a tapestry-like quality which is almost too good to be laid on the floor. Whole rooms can be carpeted in this technique. Although stretching is sometimes difficult to achieve, the effect is extremely fine and wonderful in a bedroom or private sitting room.

Chapter 3

TYPES *of* FLOORINGS *and* FLOORCOVERINGS

See Chapter 8 for guidelines on the preparation of existing floors to receive the various types of floorcoverings discussed in this chapter.

What are the trends in the use of 'hard' flooring in the home?

In many parts of Europe, as well as in tropical countries, hard flooring is commonly used in the home, especially for the ground-floor rooms. In many traditional European kitchens (which also serve as living and dining rooms), floors of quarry tiles or brick are common. In many parts of Europe the whole ground floors of many homes are tiled, then certain areas covered, typically with raffia matting and rugs, to provide softness in appropriate areas in the living rooms and bedrooms. Few bathrooms in the warmer countries are carpeted, ceramic tiles being more usual.

In Britain, until within living memory, the common flooring materials for kitchens, pantries and other ground floor rooms in many houses in country districts were stone, brick, slate or

(Right) Encaustic tiles from Provence bear a close relation to those so often found in the entrance of a Victorian house and the chancel of a church.
They have a strong traditional character, ideal where a period flavour is needed in a house and especially useful for a conservatory. (Fired Earth – Limestone.)

A natural stone floor has a feeling of quality and an established presence. This very orthodox pattern, also from Fired Earth, is easily achieved, utilizing black slate squares between the limestone slabs. It would be good to see a revival of some of the other historic patterns, together with purpose designed layouts. With special cutting it is possible to set such a pattern in perspective, thus creating the illusion of extended space – almost a Bridget Riley creation and a practical work of art to boot.

ceramic tiles. Many of these old floors were later concealed below a layer of screed, and then covered with woodblock or parquet or laid with linoleum or vinyl.

Within the last two generations, we have seen a change from the general use of linoleum for the ground floor and upper floors of typical British homes, and the more general use of carpeting. The typical home before

Fired Earth now market handmade classic terracotta tiles which introduce the warmth of the southern sun into a room. They too are the close cousin of our native floor brick or pamment. Here (left) a border tile neatly squares off the diagonal pattern before it meets the wall.

the 1939/45 War would have had linoleum in all rooms, with a carpet piece in the sitting room, and a rug in front of the fireplace in each room. Now many homes are carpeted throughout except for the kitchen, bathroom and utility room.

Traditional brick flooring is now only used for situations such as conservatories and patios. Quarry tiles and ceramic tiles are very popular in domestic premises for entrance halls, kitchens and utility rooms, ground-floor toilets etc. Woodblock (parquet) flooring can be very attractive in such areas, but is not recommended for places where there may be spillages of water, i.e. in kitchens, utility rooms and ground-floor toilets, where it is generally better to use an impervious flooring material which is hygienic and easily mopped clean. Vinyl floorcoverings which are patterned to simulate brick, tiles or parquet flooring are often used in these areas.

44

Could one consider using natural stone as a flooring material for appropriate parts of a house?

Stone was the usual material for buildings and floors in Britain for centuries. The builders used local materials such as granite, slate and limestone for flooring the kitchens, sculleries and outhouses. In some cases they used dressed stone, in others they employed cobbles or pebbles. In Scotland and the north of England, large square or rectangular blocks of dressed stone such as granite (termed 'sets') were used for floors within the house and for paving out of doors. The practice went out of use generally with the invention of improved cement and concrete in the early 19th Century. The availability of better quality cement stimulated many builders in the late 1800's to lay mosaic stone floors (terrazzo) in imitation of Italian practice. Terrazzo is seldom used in new homes because of the high cost.

If you should live in a house with natural stone flooring you might be reluctant to have it taken up (except to lay a waterproof membrane below); certainly you could consider having it re-laid, or possibly levelled, and its surface dressed by grinding. To lay new stone floors of the traditional types these days would be very expensive.

I have bought an old house with brick flooring in the kitchen. Should I have this old flooring taken up?

Rooms with traditional brick flooring are now only found in houses built in the last century or earlier. For practical reasons, brick flooring was used only on the ground floor, the upper floors usually being 'suspended' floors of wooden floorboards supported on timber joists. Some very old country cottages originally had floors made of clay or hard-packed mud which may have been overlaid with brick much later.

If you should purchase an old property with a genuine old brick floor, say, in the kitchen or pantry, do not be in a hurry to tell your builder to tear it up. Some antique brick floors are of quite beautiful colour, and could either be re-laid (with an impervious dampcourse membrane underneath) or, if they are free from all signs of damp, they can be surface-dressed by grinding to restore them most attractively to their original condition. It may be necessary to re-grout the joints. An old brick floor which is free from damp and has been surfaced dressed can be re-sealed, and could then give many years of good service.

In a kitchen a brick floor can feel cold underfoot, so it might be a good idea to put down one or two mats at places such as in front of the sink. Choose mats of colours that harmonise with the brick tones.

Brick paths are very popular in gardens. Continuing the external brick paving into a patio or conservatory is an attractive way of deliberately blurring the boundary between house and garden.

A word of caution. There are available a type of very thin bricks which are

Different geology but equally suitable for floors are large slabs of slate. Nowadays such material can be sent from all over the world, much coming from Africa. Fired Earth market this Kashmir slate which contrasts, within its strata, layers of rust brown and olive green. Special finishing liquids make it easy to keep looking fresh (left).

intended for wall-facings. These are either specially-made wafer-thin bricks or are real bricks cut into slices. These products are intended to be used purely for their decorative effect and are not suitable for use as flooring.

Has the use of linoleum gone out of fashion?

Definitely not! At present, a modern improved form of linoleum is making a big comeback, and is often specified by interior designers.

Linoleum (lino) was invented by Frederick Walton in 1863. The original material consisted of various types of natural fibre materials granulated and bound together with oils and resins hot-rolled on to a jute backing. The name 'linoleum' was coined from 'linum' (the flax plant) and 'oleum' (oil). The material was somewhat brittle but hard-wearing. In prewar England, linoleum graced the floors of both the rich and the poor. It was durable, it could be scrubbed or polished and was relatively cheap. Early lino usually had floral motifs in imitation of the popular carpet designs of the day.

Modern linoleum has a formulation mainly using natural and sustainable raw materials, such as ground cork and woodflour, with linseed oil and resins. The material is calendered onto a backing fabric and then cured at high temperature. Jute was traditionally used as the backing but modern linoleum may be backed with hession or a woven polyester material. The modern product is more flexible, less likely to crack and lays flat without curling. Linoleum should be stuck down with a recommended adhesive over its whole area; it should never be loose laid or just stuck down at the edges.

The clean, crisp quality of an Amtico floor tile brings style with hygiene to a kitchen.

What are the features of modern linoleum?

Modern lino feels fairly warm underfoot, is highly durable, has excellent indentation resistance and a degree of resilience which muffles the noise of footsteps. It has good resistance to many normal stains and even to cigarette burns – any marks can be removed by rubbing gently with a nylon scouring brush.

Linoleum is available in plain colours, or a variety of patterns. On a smooth floor elegant and interesting designs can be created by laying areas of different colours. Borders are available. Properly laid, the butted joins are imperceptible and, if required, the seams can be welded to make them watertight. Linoleum can be washed and polished but it is important to ensure that water does not get under it for this could cause rotting of the backing. For this reason, the edges and seams should be made watertight.

The 'Marmoleum' linoleum product from Forbo-Nairn Ltd has a 'marble effect' design that goes right through the product and therefore keeps its looks. As it is resistant to fading by sunlight, it is suitable for use in conservatories provided it is laid on a suitable subfloor.

Forbo-Nairn (who are the only British manufacturers of linoleum and who have been making it for over 100 years) recommend that linoleum should always be laid by a skilled craftsman. They may be able to recommend a contractor to you, or you can ask the Contract Flooring Association to do this.

Is rubber flooring a practical option for homes?

Rubber flooring can be made non slip by incorporating raised discs into the design. Modern interior designers love it for its originality. You could love it too as a comfortable surface in a kitchen or bathroom. This flooring is by Schaeffer.

Modern rubber flooring is extensively used in hospitals and in other locations where a resilient and hygienic floorcovering that muffles footfalls is required. In such applications the seams can be sealed for hygiene. Because it is more difficult to lay, and more costly than linoleum or vinyl, its use in homes is limited. It could be difficult to find a flooring contractor willing to lay the small area that you would require in your home. DIY laying of rubber flooring is not recommended.

However rubber floor tiles are a practical form of flooring and easy to lay. The floor to which they are applied must be smooth and flat and a special adhesive must be used. The surface of the tiles may be textured to reduce the risk of slipping. Rubber flooring is usually made in muted plain colours but some patterned tiles are available.

What are the general qualities of vinyl floorcoverings?

Although linoleum has made quite a comeback in recent years for kitchens etc and as a designer material, vinyl is a competitor both to linoleum and to flooring materials made of natural rubber and synthetic rubber-like materials for home use.

A tiled floor can only be laid successfully on a hard base (e.g. cement or concrete) and cannot generally be laid on the suspended upper floors of ordinary houses unless the floor is free of bounce or has been specially stiffened. However, you will probably be able to find a vinyl product (tiles or sheet) that will realistically simulate virtually any kind of hard flooring you may have in mind.

What types of vinyl floorcoverings are available?

The range of vinyl floorcoverings is enormous and they come in an amazing variety of colours, patterns and forms (including cushion vinyls) which make them highly versatile and adaptable. The better-quality vinyl products will give many years of satisfactory service in domestic situations. Vinyl has been described as the chameleon of floorcoverings, for ingenious manufacturers have created vinyl products that convincingly mimic materials such as marble, granite, ceramic tiles, brick, woodblock flooring, parquet and planked floors etc, even providing these products with appropriate surface textures.

The price you pay for vinyl will reflect the wearing quality of the product. For economy some vinyl products are manufactured as composite materials, they have a thin layer of high pvc content material on the surface and a backing of lower grade material which may have a mineral filler. One range of vinyls contains minute particles of quartz embedded in their surface layer to improve resistance to slipping and wear. Another version has a layer of clear vinyl on its surface, laid over a coloured or patterned layer. There are also many varieties of cushion vinyls.

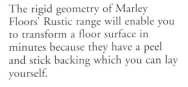

The rigid geometry of Marley Floors' Rustic range will enable you to transform a floor surface in minutes because they have a peel and stick backing which you can lay yourself.

By contrast Marley Floors' Sigma collection suggests a hint of Turkish delight.

Computer controlled cutting machines create an infinite variety of shapes to be assembled which interlock to form a neatly fitting floor. This stunning pattern from DLW Floorings is one which would transform a dull cubic room to mind blowing proportions. Both linoleum and PVC material can be used – and you can even get your name written into the surface.

The imitative nature of plastic flooring enables the makers to focus in on socially desirable patterns, such as this woodblock flooring design. Freed from imitation such floors could take off into interstellar space as far as the imagination is concerned, but often such way out designs fit ill with other objects around the house. (Nairn Cushionflor.)

Other Marley patterns, like Delta shown here, enable an infinite variety in matching to other colours and surface materials. Sheet materials are ideal for bathrooms.

What are cushion vinyl floorcoverings?

Composite vinyl floorcoverings (cushion vinyls) have a pvc foam backing to improve their resilience underfoot. These are sometimes described as 'acoustic quality', but note that while the backing will muffle the sound of footsteps (both in the room and as heard in the room below), it does not greatly affect the sound level of other noises transmitted through the floor. According to its thickness and quality, the foam backing will reduce the sensation of cold coming up to one's feet from a cold underfloor, and will contribute to the heat insulation between an upstairs room where it is installed and the room below it.

What are the main features of quarry tiles for flooring?

Quarry tiles are a traditional form of tile produced by firing the reddish brown clay from certain quarries. They are generally machine-made though rather costly handmade quarry tiles are available. Because quarry tiles are fired at a higher temperature than terracotta or ceramic tiles, they are tough and dense. Because they are non-porous they are impervious to moisture; hence they do not easily stain and are frostproof. Quarry tiles are self-coloured according to the colour of the clay from which they are made and are usually of red or reddish brown colour. Note that the colour may vary from batch to batch or even within a batch.

Quarry tiles might be described as a slightly coarser product than ceramic tiles. They are extremely hard-wearing and less likely to crack than ceramic tiles. They have a matt anti-slip surface which may be smooth or textured. Machine-made quarries are laid in a cement-based adhesive and are suitable for indoor and outdoor use.

There are handmade quarry tiles in square, rectangular and octagonal shapes. The octagonal shape may be used to create some interesting patterns. If laid in parallel rows, small squares are left where four tiles meet. If the octagonal tiles are laid in diagonal lines, the open squares at the intersections are larger. Many interesting variations on the theme are possible; for example, the open squares can be filled in with small quarry tiles of a different colour, or with small coloured or patterned ceramic tiles, to produce a wide range of pattern effects.

Handmade quarry tiles may be slightly variable in dimensions and thickness. Because both handmade and machine-made quarry tiles are difficult to cut to size, laying them requires some skill.

What are the main features of terracotta tiles?

The word terracotta means 'cooked earth'. Such tiles have been made since the earliest times of ancient civilisation, when man first discovered that clay becomes hard when it is fired. Generally similar in appearance to handmade quarry tiles, terracotta tiles are distinguished by their rich colours.

Terracotta floor tiles are generally imported from Spain or South America and have features which are a combination of quarry tiles and ordinary ceramic floor tiles. They may not be completely impervious to moisture. They may be handmade or machine-made. Some handmade terracotta tiles seem to be quite crudely made – but that is part of their charm! Terracotta wall tiles may be glazed but generally floor tiles are unglazed. They come in reddish or honey colours and the colour may not be constant within a batch – or even within a tile, for some have interesting grain effects due to a mixture of clays. Terracotta tiles need buffing after they are laid.

Terracotta tiles are more porous than quarry tiles and may need to be sealed with linseed oil or a proprietary sealant to prevent unsightly staining after the floor is laid (but note that quarry tiles and unglazed ceramic tiles should not be sealed in an attempt to reduce soiling – see Chapter 8) .

(Right) So great is the appeal of a natural flooring material that ceramic tile makers find it worthwhile to imitate the effect of stone in the surface finish of their tiles. This 'Naturefloor' by Pilkington's Tiles is produced in large scale elements which complete the geological allusion.

Such is the market appeal of old floor tiles that Fired Earth are able to retrieve used examples and recycle them. The result is an effect of instant antiquity. Note that the surface has been sealed for easy upkeep.

What are the main features of ceramic tiles for flooring?

Ceramic tiles come in two varieties, i.e. wall tiles and floor tiles. Floor tiles are graded according to their abrasion-resistance and are available unglazed, although glazed tiles are more usually used for domestic flooring. They are produced in white and a wide range of colours as well as in patterned designs. It is important to note

that the colour of ceramic tiles may vary from batch to batch so that additional tiles bought after your first purchase may not exactly match the colour of those bought previously.

Ceramic floor tiles are very hard-wearing, are easy to keep clean and do not need sealing; however they are brittle and a tile may crack if something heavy is dropped on it (a cooking pot, say). Ceramic tiles are quite difficult to trim and cut to fit round pipes and other obstructions. The standard sizes of floor tiles range from 4in x 4in (100mm x 100mm) up to 15 3/4in x 15 3/4in (400mm x 400mm) and both square and rectangular tiles are available.

Ceramic floor tiling is very popular for kitchens, utility rooms, bathrooms, conservatories and patios. Not all grades are frostproof, so if planning to use them in a conservatory or for a patio or outdoor path, check their suitability for the proposed application with your supplier.

While it may be necessary to replace linoleum and vinyl flooring after a period of time, a well-laid ceramic tiled floor will probably last a lifetime, and retain its good looks more or less indefinitely.

In the same way that carpets can be made in imitation of antique patterns, ceramic tiles too can draw on inspiration in their design from ancient precedent. In this chequerboard layout, created by Alex Zdankowicz, the starting point were tiles from the 14th-century Popes' Palace at Avignon. The glazed terracotta tiles sing out with an orison of devices and clear Provençal colours.

A variation of the single square floor tile pattern is to introduce a framing tile to contrast between a group of four, thus creating a larger scaled pattern. (All this spread, Paris Ceramics.)

Is it possible to lay ceramic tiles on a wooden suspended floor?

Yes. Quarry tiles can be used this way but, in some cases, it will be necessary to stiffen the floor by overlaying it first with stout composition boarding such as marine plywood. A special flexible fixing adhesive must be used, such as Quarrylastic (TM) from Dennis Ruabon Ltd. If the floor is likely to be wetted, see the next question.

Could I incorporate a shower area in my tiled-floor bathroom?

Provided the tiles are correctly installed, grouted with a waterproof grout and **cove base skirting tiles** are correctly installed at the walls, yes. However, this is not recommended for a shower installed on a wooden suspended floor or above ground level, where a shower tray should be used. Glazed ceramic tiles can be slippery underfoot, especially when wet, so, for any 'wet barefoot' areas, the use of anti-slip tiles is recommended. To ensure that the installation is watertight, and to prevent damage from wetting the floor too early, it is recommended that a newly tiled shower area should not be used for at least two weeks after the completion of the tiling.

Even more polished is the effect achieved with inlaid mosaics. The Romans did it to perfection and their floors have lasted until today. This hallway looks set to last a thousand years too.

What is mosaic tiling?

A mosaic floor consists of tiny ceramic tiles of various colours, either cast to size or chipped from larger tiles, the pieces being set into a bed of cement. By selection of the colours, decorative patterns (or even pictures!) can be formed. Not to be confused with terrazzo, mosaic tiling in ancient times was an artform as well as a means of laying an impervious floor. It was extensively used by the ancient Greeks and by the Romans.

The concept is still popular today, and factory-made mosaic tiles may be purchased in panels, with the pieces composed in a pattern and adhering to a backing sheet of paper or woven material, ready to be planted into the cement screed.

(Terrazzo paving differs from mosaic by being comprised not of tiles but of tiny chips of marble or other stone similarly set into cement and the surface then ground smooth and level.)

Is laying tiles a job that the average DIY-er can tackle successfully?

Most people who have DIY skills seem to manage to fix wall tiles quite successfully, but laying a ceramic tiled floor can present problems with which the inexperienced amateur may not be able to cope with. Even with the use of 'self-levelling cement', those unskilled in the art may find it difficult to get a truly level floor. If the surface screed is not supported by a really firm foundation, cracks will inevitably appear after a time. Some tile suppliers, such as Fired Earth, provide excellent instruction booklets on the techniques of designing and laying tiled floors and there is plenty of information in the relevant DIY books (see Appendix 1). For durability, floor tiles should be laid to comply with the technical and quality requirements of British Standard 5385. Unless you are skilled and experienced in tile laying, you may prefer to have your flooring laid by a professional. The National Master Tile Fixers Association (see Appendix 3) can put you in touch with a suitable contractor who may be able to guide you on the selection of tiling materials or even design a floor to your requirements. It is recommended that you talk with the tile fixer before you buy your tiles.

Cork floor tiles from Westco have excellent qualities both in softness to walk on and as sound deadening by reducing impact sound transmission. The modern vinyl surfaces given to some tiles make them easy to wipe over and clean, whilst the natural quality of the cork reads much better than a printed-on design.

What are the characteristics of cork tile flooring?

A floor covered in cork tiles is warm to touch; its surface is resilient so that footsteps are quiet. Cork tiles usually come in the familiar colour of natural cork. Unless they are sealed with a hard glossy varnish, cork tiles present a surface which is not slippery.

There are two grades of cork tiles: the thin grade which is intended for decorative use on walls and the heavy duty, tougher grade which is suitable for flooring. Unsealed natural cork tiles are absorbent and will need to be sealed with polyurethane varnish after they have been laid. There are also cork tiles available which have been sealed during manufacture these may have a matt or semi-gloss anti-slip finish.

Cork tiles are made in a range of sizes, a popular size being 300mm (12 inches) square. They must be laid on a smooth, flat floor surface and fixed with an adhesive. Some tiles of this kind are supplied with a self-adhesive backing applied during manufacture.

Is there still a place for natural wood flooring in the home?

Modern laying techniques enable hardwood floors to go down without seeing the fixings, which can be by a clip method or by secret nailing through the tongue of the tongued-and-grooved edge. Here, an 8mm wide beech boarded floor warmly reflects light in this attic conversion in London's Regent's Park. (Junckers.)

Ordinary square edged boarded wooden floors (i.e. those which are not composed of tongued-and-grooved boards) can result in chilly draughts rising between the boards and sound being too easily transmitted between rooms. But, if you have a well-laid wooden floor with tongued-and-grooved boards, you could consider having it sanded and sealed. If the colour is not to your liking, the floor could be stained before it is sealed.

Alternatively, the floor could be attractively improved by being overlaid with tongued-and-grooved hardwood boarding, or overlaid with parquet flooring.

Parquet flooring can also be laid on to concrete floors.

There is great pleasure to be gained from having a real hardwood floor. In a world in which we are often confronted by replicas of natural things rather than the natural materials themselves, a real timber floor, such as maple, beech, oak, ash or pine is an aesthetic treat. If you are concerned with the conservation aspects of this use of wood, you will be glad to know that some leading producers of solid hardwood flooring follow the conservationist principle in that they plant a new tree for every one they cut down.

The tongued-and-grooved wooden planks can be stuctural, i.e. they replace the original softwood floorboards, or a thinner grade of tongued-and-grooved planking may be laid over the exsisting floorboards.

Such flooring is ideal in a music room because the reflection of sound from the wood floor lengthens the period of reverberation. Any necessary dampening of the reverberation can easily be achieved by the use of rugs. The combination of a beautiful wood floor and beautiful rugs will be a visual pleasure too.

The ash flooring shown here contrasts white and brown heartwood with flamey grain to create a surface with the quality of a modern painting and providing the main decorative detail of the room shown. The timber is solid and tough and provides an ideal sounding-board for music. (Kährs.)

Regarding flooring and floorcoverings, are there any awful mistakes that one might make?

Yes, there are a few. For example:

◆ Don't lay ceramic tiles of any kind in a conservatory or on a patio without checking if the product you have chosen is frost-resistant.

◆ Don't lay vinyl tiles or vinyl flooring over a floor which has cracks or uneven areas in it (they will show through when the vinyl beds down). In bad cases it may be necessary to fit a layer of hardboard or floor grade chipboard to present a smooth surface for the vinyl.

◆ Don't lay new vinyl floor products over existing vinyl flooring products.

◆ Don't lay thin, wall-quality ceramic tiles or thin brick forms as flooring (they will soon crack).

◆ Don't drag heavy items of furniture which have metal 'domes of silence' on their feet across linoleum, vinyl or any kind of hard flooring (you will scratch or mark the flooring).

◆ Don't order your new flooring until you have checked your choice of colour by bringing home the largest available samples to see in your room (see Chapter 1 on the pitfalls of not checking the colour properly).

◆ Don't overlay existing woodblock flooring with an impervious material such as vinyl with the air excluded, the woodblock material may rot.

◆ Don't lay woodblock on a poorly waterproofed solid base.

Chapter 4

CHOOSING *Carpets, Floorings and Floorcoverings*

How does one start to choose between carpeting and other types of flooring for any situation?

When deciding about flooring, you must take into account practical considerations and your specific needs. Of all the surfaces in the room, it is the floor that is used the most. Your flooring is not just decorative; it is a functional surface which must firstly guarantee safety, i.e. be unlikely to cause an accident by someone tripping or slipping; it must provide a degree of comfort appropriate to the function of the room and it should be hygienic and resist wear. Perhaps you will require the flooring to provide some sound or heat insulation. In a kitchen or bathroom, you will require the flooring to be water-resistant; the flooring of a busy entrance hall that gets lots of traffic should be hard-wearing and easy to keep clean.

In making that first big choice between carpet and hard flooring, remember that the floor is the only room surface with which you regularly come into contact. Babies learn to crawl on the carpet; toddlers take their first uncertain steps on the carpet. Older children seem to spend a great deal of time sprawled on the carpet, playing or watching TV. In some homes, it is quite usual for adults and children alike to sit on the carpet; you may be sure they would not be so keen to sit on a hard floor!

On the other hand, hard flooring offers the advantages of being hygienic, easy to clean and long-lasting. Not all hard floorings are cold to the touch; cork tiles, for example. In Chapter 3 we review some of the enormous range of hard flooring materials and floorcoverings other than carpet. There is a wide range of possibilities your choice must take account of practical requirements, aesthetic considerations and cost. Although carpets are the most popular floorcovering for the living room, bedrooms, and stairs, you might wish to consider other flooring materials such as wood, woodblock, ceramic tiles, and floor coverings such as vinyl, cork and linoleum for the other rooms. These present a hygienic surface, and may be

A pre-sealed hardwood floor creates no dust to which people may be allergic. Junckers pre-sealed floors are available in oak, ash, beech and elm, either as a structural floor in 22mm thick boards or as an overlay floor, 8 or 12mm thick.

considered preferable for the rooms used by a child or adult who is sensitive to dusts (see the notes on house dust mites in Appendix 2).

I may be moving to a new home soon. How might this affect my choice of carpeting or flooring?

How long you expect to be occupying the premises is an important and practical factor of choice. It is well known that making improvements to a home, such as putting in new flooring to a kitchen, is unlikely to affect the price you get for the house when the time comes to sell. If you are a tenant, you may be reluctant to put down flooring which you cannot take with you at some time in the future, and this may lead you to choose carpeting rather than hard flooring. Carpet pieces can simply be rolled up and moved without any problems. If the rooms in your new home are smaller, it is possible to take up wall-to-wall carpeting and lay it in your new home, but this may not be successful if the carpet is visibly worn or faded.

How should one set about making the big decision of choosing the colour of carpet or floorcovering?

When looking at samples of carpets and floorcovering in the showroom, we may start by looking at the colours and patterns, trying to imagine how they would look in the room for which we are buying the carpet.

If you have understood the principle of 'colour adaptation' which we discussed in Chapter 1, you will appreciate that you cannot judge a colour by looking only at a small sample, for you will doubtless be colour-adapted to the other colours around you. A successful colour scheme for a room will contain colours which may either match, harmonise or complement each other. There is an infinite number of possible colour combinations which achieve this, and also many that won't!

Choosing a carpet of a single plain colour may make your decisions a little easier by reducing your number of choices. Patterned carpets have their own special charms (not the least of which is their ability not to show dirt!), but you must choose with great care. It should not be too difficult to find a patterned carpet which pleases you and which embodies the right combination of colours. Some carpet manufacturers offer plain and patterned carpets in dozens of different colourways.

When you go to look at carpets or floorcoverings, take with you the largest possible samples of coloured materials from your room – curtaining, wallpaper, loose-covers etc. Put them beside the products in the showroom, and try to see them both in natural light and electric light. Select a few 'possibles', and ask to borrow the largest available samples to take home to look at again in your room. To avoid an expensive mistake, take your time over this important choice.

Plain or patterned? There is often too great a choice in carpet designs. You may need to be ruthlessly selective. Left and below, two similar rooms indicate the main contrasts. You don't need to be Scottish to enjoy the neutral toned plaid carpet from Stoddard Templeton which provides an instant key to the character of the room – all stripped pine and natural finishes.

Left, by way of contrast, the overtly Victorian decoration of the adjoining bedroom with its intricate turned and crocheted detail is given a calming influence by the all-over plainness of a well constructed Brintons carpet from the Palace Velvet range.

Is there one kind of carpet that will suit everyone?

No. Some properties of carpets may be more important to you than others. For example, you may be seeking an economical carpet that has improved resistance to soiling (i.e. to the effects of accumulated dust and dirt through everyday use). Or you might decide that, because there is going to be heavy foot traffic on the carpet (say, in an entrance hall, or along a passage that gets a lot of traffic), resistance to wear is the most important factor of choice. You will remember that a darker shade of carpet is less prone to the 'shading' effect due to pile flattening, and that patterned carpets do not show up small stains in the way that unpatterned carpets do. Your choice may favour a pattern with large features, or a pattern composed of small elements that visually blend into an overall general impression of a colour. Strongly coloured oriental patterns, for example, might look quite out of place in a small modern flat with light-coloured furniture, but would look most appropriate in a large room with traditional or period furniture.

There are no rigid rules on how to choose a carpet. Virtually any type, colour or pattern of carpet that takes your fancy could give you many years of satisfaction. However, one does hear of people who have had second thoughts when they saw their new carpet in position, and later felt the need to change their curtains or put new covers on their upholstered furniture in order to achieve a more harmonious effect.

In selecting a carpet, what should we look for?

The decorative effect of your new carpet will be an important factor in your choice. In the showroom, you will be seeking certain colours or patterns that you think will best suit your particular room and your decor as we discussed in Chapter 1. However, there are also many factors of quality to be considered. By studying the examples given in this book, and – more importantly – looking at and handling samples in the showroom and discussing them with the salesman, you may choose the product that will most closely meet all your requirements and your pocket.

Just looking at colours and patterns does not tell us everything about the carpet samples; we also have a quite natural desire to touch them to judge their texture.

If we like the feel of a carpet in the showroom, can we rely upon our judgement as to its quality?

No. A poor quality carpet may present well in the showroom; but after six months of wear the pile may be flattened and have lost much of its bounce. A good quality carpet feels good to begin with, and carries on feeling good (if you look after it properly) for many years.

Without experience, we cannot easily make sound judgements of carpet quality. The quality features of a carpet relate to such factors as colourfastness, resistance to soiling and stains, resistance to flattening of the pile and – of course – durability. When we have looked at and handled samples of various types of carpets, we will start to appreciate how they differ in their texture and in the thickness of the pile, and also how well the pile recovers after it has been compressed. To make really sound decisions, we must look at the backing of the carpet, and inspect the label that describes the product.

What can we learn from the label on the back of the carpet?

The labelling on the back of the carpet samples that you see in the showroom should contain the essential information called for in British Standard 3655, including the manufacturer's advice regarding the rooms of the house for which the carpet is suitable, e.g. living room, dining room, kitchen, bedroom, bathroom, hall and stairs. The carpet manufacturer may have his own distinctive label which will contain useful information about the product, including:

◆ The method of construction e.g. tufted, woven (Axminster or Wilton) or bonded.

◆ What the pile materials are e.g. wool, a man-made fibre (nylon, acrylic, rayon, polypropylene etc) or a mixture of wool and man-made fibre.

◆ The widths available (note that Imperial and metric widths are listed in Appendix 3 of this book).

◆ Suitability for use, recommendations (the manufacturer's recommendations as to the rooms in the home for which the carpet is suitable).

As well as taking note of the manufacturer's recommendations, it is useful to have the advice of your retailer. You should also look for the label of the BCMA Carpet Grading Scheme which has a distinctive logo.

What is the BCMA Carpet Grading Scheme?

This is the grading scheme operated by the British Carpet Manufacturers' Association (BCMA) which is used by major carpet producers in the United Kingdom. The scheme is based on British Standard 7131:1989, and offers consumers:

◆ independent checking of pile fibre weight and density;

◆ machine testing of the carpet's ability to keep its 'as new' look;

◆ random testing to maintain quality standards; and,

◆ a room suitability guide.

The BCMA classification of the carpet may be shown on a separate label, or the information may be incorporated into the manufacturer's label.

The BCMA Grading Scheme ensures that the carpet has been independently checked in accordance with a number of British Standard tests. These tests take account of the form of construction of the carpet, the type of pile material, the weight and density of the pile and its height above the backing.

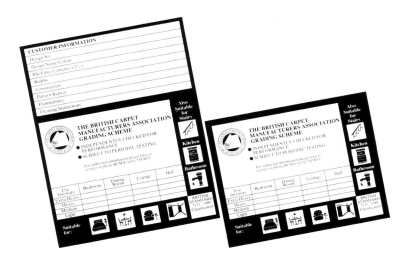

If you have any problem regarding the labelling of carpets with which the retailer cannot help you, you can phone BCMA (tel: 0171 580 7155) for additional information.

How might one set about choosing a type of hard flooring or floorcovering?

It is unlikely that a householder would choose a relatively costly form of hard flooring if their tenure of the property was expected to be brief. Expertly laid, good quality hardwood floors or ceramic tiled floors are likely to last a lifetime; but you may have to be content with a good quality vinyl surface that imitates the fine timber floor or the ceramic tiled floor you would have liked to purchase. In any case, excellent quality modern vinyl floorcoverings are actually preferred by many people to the materials that they mimic!

In general, people in rented accommodation tend to choose lower-cost floorings or to buy carpeting or carpet pieces that can be taken to their new home some time in the future. A good compromise is to put down a type of flooring that is not as expensive as a good quality fitted carpet or natural wood flooring; for example, you could put down carpet tiles or cork tiles. Even so, many good suppliers will provide the right technical advice on what materials to use as well as give the purchaser plenty of simple-to-follow guidance, making it possible for a skilled do-it-yourselfer to undertake techniques thought by some to be only possible by professional floor-layers.

A handsome hardwood floor can also provide the key to the decor of a traditionally designed room, as in this example of Napoli oak boarding by Kährs (UK) Ltd.

Could I save money by laying carpeting or floorcoverings myself?

If you really have the skills, or if you can get some expert guidance or tuition, yes. But, let us review the possibilities:

◆ **Wall-to-wall carpeting.** Laying of tufted and woven carpeting is strictly a job for a skilled carpet layer. However, you might be able to follow detailed instructions and have a go at it; but if, your carpet should later prove to be unsatisfactory in some way, e.g. not being properly stretched, you might find that the carpet supplier would be reluctant to help. Remember: Laying a carpet is easy; but fitting a carpet is a job for the professional!

◆ **Kitchen carpet.** Flocked kitchen carpet seems to be one form of carpeting that amateurs may be able to lay more easily. This is recognised by the makers; for example, Bonar & Flotex Ltd issue clear DIY instructions for laying their 'Flotex' kitchen carpet, and it would appear from their literature that self-laid carpet still qualifies for their Ten Year Guarantee provided that the product is properly installed.

(Note that the following flooring materials can only be stuck down to a dry subfloor.)

◆ **Linoleum and Vinyl flooring.** Laying linoleum or vinyl flooring (including cushion vinyls) from the roll is a job for a professional, so DIY laying is not recommended. However, laying a small area of lino tiles or vinyl tiles might not prove to be too difficult if the subfloor is really smooth and flat. Obtain the maker's instructions, and follow them carefully, noting that some adhesives give off flammable or irritating vapours, and that some people are sensitive to the chemicals in adhesives.

◆ **Cork tiles.** As a visit to your local DIY store will show, cork tiles are a popular form of flooring for amateurs to attempt. It is worth while buying good quality tiles of the thicker variety, and to take the trouble to read and follow carefully the manufacturer's instructions, again noting that some adhesives give off flammable or irritating vapours, and that some people are sensitive to the chemicals in adhesives. Some cork flooring tiles are provided with an adhesive backing protected with a layer of peel-off paper or plastic film.

For an 'instant' floor surface that will stand up to everything a teenager could throw at it, a Marley cushioned Bellair design comes ready to peel and stick down.

◆ **Ceramic tiles.** Some manufacturers provide detailed fixing instructions for DIY. However, you might prefer to employ a professional for tiling of an upstairs suspended floor or for tiling a bathroom or other room in which wetting of the floor is likely. If you are going to get professional help with fixing ceramic tiles, it is recommended that you consult with the tile-fixer before you purchase the tiles, and don't just present him with the tiles to lay. Ask for his guidance on what type of tile and where to buy them. Indeed, many reputable tile-fixers will actually supply the tiles – often with a saving to the user.

◆ **Natural timber flooring.** Hardwood flooring is available in thicknesses of 22mm, 20mm, 15mm, 12mm and 8mm. It is recommended that enthusiastic amateurs should approach this subject very cautiously. Laying 22mm structural timber flooring is strictly for professionals, whereas laying an 8mm overlay timber floor should be within the capacity of a dedicated amateur who sets about this DIY task with application and care.

For a sense of sheer quality in hall or conservatory, Paris Ceramics can provide limestone flags with black cabochons set at the corners. It's timeless and very smart.

◆ **Woodblock and mosaic panel flooring.** Overlay flooring in these materials, laid on a sound, dry and firm underfloor, may be successfully attempted by fairly skilled DIY-ers; but the biggest problems will be sanding, polishing and sealing (for which the professional is better equipped as well as experienced).

◆ **Natural floorcoverings.** Laying less than room-size pieces of natural floorcoverings (e.g. woven materials in grasses, jute, coir and sisal) should not present great problems. But laying such materials wall-to-wall or on stairs might merit the employment of a professional layer. Information on this is available from suppliers such as Fired Earth.

It is almost essential to have a natural timber floor as a background for a good modern rug. The unpretentious quality of the wood provides the perfect foil for bright colours. (Junckers.)

As the years go by the quality of the ash floor, here laid in a roof lit sun room by Junckers, will continue to mature and improve.

A happy and enlightened combination of surface finishes make this interior sing. Eclecticism is the hallmark of a personal taste, which here combines Iznik wall tiles, natural woven coir matting, flat weave designs and a multi-coloured carpet from Fired Earth into a glorious and cosy nook.

A softer surface for bare feet, more
suitable for a bedroom, is achieved
by using a bleached Jute flooring
laid over a good haircord underfelt.
(Both on this page from Fired
Earth.)

Herringbone twill weave to a
coconut mat make a distinguished
background for a serious study.

How can I get in touch with professional carpet-fitters and flooring contractors?

Refer to Part 1 of Appendix 4, where the relevant professional and trade associations are listed. All of these will welcome your enquiry and provide you with information or help you to locate suitable suppliers or contractors.

Are there any problems in choosing rugs?

Hardly any. If you like the look of a rug and buy it, unless you are buying at the very top of the range you will not have spent a great deal. And if, when you get it home, you are not too pleased with the design or colour, just put it aside; sooner or later you'll find just the place for it!

Rugs are currently very popular. Many are surprisingly cheap and yet really attractive and colourful. Perhaps this is why people have recently started giving rugs as presents – and not only to newlyweds. It is almost impossible to give anyone the wrong rug; if it doesn't suit one room, it will probably look fine in another.

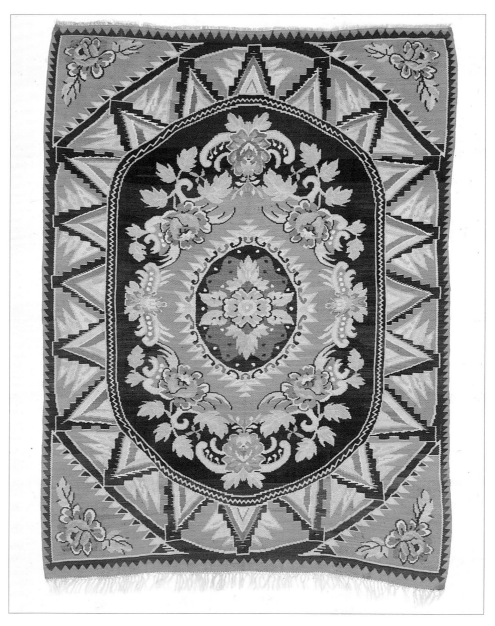

If you have a valuable rug like this one from Robert Stevenson Oriental Carpets, it needs careful cleaning.

Part 2

FITTING AND CARING FOR CARPETS, FLOORING AND FLOORCOVERINGS

Chapter 5

PREPARATIONS *before your new* CARPET *or* FLOORING
is laid

If I were to order my new carpet on the basis of my own measurements of the room, is it likely that there would be problems?

Yes! By all means make your own preliminary sketch and take some measurements so that you can get an idea of quantity and cost; but, before you order the carpet, it is essential to **have the room measured by a professional carpet planner**. He will know about the available widths of your chosen carpet (and the tolerances on them). He will know how to plan the job so that the carpet can be laid with the fewest possible joins – or none. He will know how to position any joins to be inconspicuous and away from areas of heaviest wear. He will allow for any waste occasioned by ensuring that the pattern matches at the joins. He will measure your room accurately, noting if corners are not exactly square, or if the walls are not exactly parallel to each other, and he will ensure that the pile direction is constant.

All reputable carpet retailers will quote you a price on a 'supply and fit' basis; thus, it becomes the responsibility of the supplier to ensure that you get a quality job, and measurement becomes entirely his responsibility.

How might the quality of the workmanship relating to the fitting of a carpet affect my satisfaction with it?

There is a saying that a carpet which has been laid by a plumber or an accountant will look like a carpet which has been laid by a plumber or an accountant! Many DIY home owners can make quite a success of laying carpet tiles; but fitting a carpet is a really skilled job. Of course, if you do have the skills, DIY fitting of your carpets is feasible; but the cost of employing a professional carpet fitter is usually well justified, and will represent only a small proportion of your total outlay on your carpet. All reputable carpet retailers will arrange for your rooms to be measured and for your carpet to be laid by a competent tradesman. If there is any difficulty in locating a suitable professional for this job, contact the National Institute of Carpet Fitters (the address is in Appendix 4).

My boarded floor is somewhat uneven. Would this harm my carpet?

While a small degree of unevenness might do no harm (especially if a substantial underlay was used), unevenness of the floor generally tends to shorten the life of a carpet. In Chapter 8 we discuss how to achieve a smooth floor surface to permit the laying of various kinds of timber floorcoverings and hard flooring, and this advice is equally applicable to creating a suitable floor on which to fit a carpet. The use of a good quality needlefelt underlay may ameliorate the problem.

Is it necessary to have an underlay under my carpet?

Except in the case of carpet tiles or 'stuck-down' carpet, the recommendation in all other cases is, yes. The underlay gives mechanical protection to the carpet, reducing the likelihood of it becoming marked due to any small unevenness of the floor. If the carpet is to be laid on a concrete floor, a good quality underlay will add valuable thermal insulation, reducing the heat-loss into the floor by as much as 50 percent and thereby making the room warmer and cheaper to heat. To some extent an underlay will reduce the amount of sound transmission through a suspended wooden floor, principally by softening the sound of footfalls. It also gives extra resilience to the carpet, making it feel more luxurious and comfortable. If you use a good quality underlay, the life and good looks of your carpet can be extended by up to 30 percent.

It is well worth discussing the matter of underlays with your carpet supplier or carpet fitter. There is a range of qualities, thickness and materials, and you may need advice as to the best underlay to go with the type of carpet you have chosen, taking into account the nature of your floor. You should select an underlay which has good flame retardant property such as is exhibited by the new generation of needlefelt underlays. A felt or foam underlay creates an extra layer between a woven-back carpet and the floor, allowing for the passage of air; this increases the effectiveness of vacuum-cleaning, giving a further increase in life and appearance detention for your carpet.

What must be done when fitting carpet, or laying hard flooring or floorcovering on a suspended wooden floor?

First refer to Chapter 8 regarding actions to be taken to bring suspended wooden floors into good condition.

When fitting carpet on a suspended wooden floor, it is recommended that a layer of paper lining is placed beneath the whole of the underlay, extending to under the skirting-board sealer. The best paper for the job would be sisal paper or thick brown paper, but even two or three layers of newspaper would be quite effective. This will prevent unsightly soiling of the carpet by dust carried by draughts of air which pass through the gaps between the floorboards. It is important to ensure that the paper extends under the skirting board and that the carpet fits neatly to the skirting board.

Before the work of laying a new hard floor, carpet or floorcovering starts, check that the skirting boards are in good condition and fit well. If the skirting boards need repainting, this should be done before a new carpet is laid. (See Chapter 8 regarding draughts which can enter a room under a badly-fitting skirting). If you have cables, electric points or telephone points etc which are mounted low down on your skirting boards, these may have to be repositioned by an electrician or telephone engineer so that the new carpet or flooring can be fitted neatly right up to the skirting without damaging them.

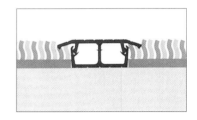

To save having costly changes to my electric wiring and telephone points, would it be possible to lay the cables under a carpet?

Wiring of any kind should not be laid under any kind of floorcovering other than carpet. It is not recommended to place any mains-voltage electric wiring under a carpet other than special cables having a flat construction and made specifically for this application. Electric cables laid under the carpet should be routed around the edges of the room to avoid accidental damage or penetration, and not placed under any area of heavy foot traffic. If there is a lift-out panel for access to cables or other services under the floor, the use of carpet tiles would permit inconspicuous access through the carpet.

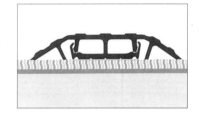

Before the carpet-fitter comes, think about any telephone cables or leads to hi-fi speakers which may have to be concealed. Telephone connections can be readily extended with plug-in extension leads. Telephone cables and leads to hi-fi speakers should preferably be run along or behind the skirting boards, but could be laid under the carpet if they can be routed away from any area of heavy foot traffic. Small diameter telephone and hi-fi speaker cables can be routed across a doorway by placing them under the gripper channel at the threshold, but other arrangements should be made for electric power cables.

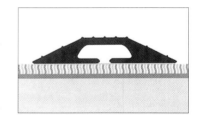

Gradus Clip-top cable ducts are ideal for running the telephone or TV aerial cable across a door threshold. Particularly useful when you have two different carpets each side of the door, as the flexible PVC duct cover will seal the edges of each side. Fitting can be by double-sided tape direct to a hard floor surface. A variety of colours are available.

What can be done to reduce wear on a stair carpet?

Heavy wear can occur at the nosings of stairs which are covered in carpeting or natural floorcoverings such as woven coir. It is essential to use a good quality hair or needlefelt underfelt. An extra length of the carpet or floorcovering material should

Most, if not all of the fittings needed in connection with laying carpet are made by Gradus Ltd., including the stair rods shown here.

also be provided at the top and bottom of each flight to permit the carpet or material to be shifted periodically and to even out wear. (Ask your professional carpet fitter to advise you on the best method of doing this.)

In old houses, a common cause of wear on the stairs is that the nosings of the treads have been damaged, and sharp areas cut through the carpet or floorcovering at this point of greatest wear. Before fitting new carpet or floorcovering, check the nosings. If any are damaged, they could be repaired by replacing the nosing mouldings.

This would be a good time to have any squeaky stairs dealt with. If there is the slightest movement in the treads, this will accelerate wear on your carpet or floorcovering, and should be corrected before the new material is laid. If you can get access to the underside of the staircase, any loose wedges should be tapped in firmly, and any glue-blocks that are missing or loose should be replaced or re-glued. If you cannot get access to the underside of the staircase, the application of some carefully positioned countersunk screws may do the trick.

How could I arrange to have a carpet piece surrounded by a hard-flooring border?

As an alternative to having carpet or floorcovering laid wall-to-wall, you could opt for a carpet piece. (We call it a 'piece' rather than a square, as they are rarely exactly square.) This has the advantages that it can be readily taken to your new home if you move, and also that the piece can be turned through 90 degrees occasionally to even up the wear.

Ask your carpet retailer to advise you on the sizes of pieces that are available in your chosen style of carpet or floorcovering, remembering that you could choose a plain or patterned piece fitted with a border joined on all sides. It would then be necessary to choose a suitable treatment for the uncovered border around the room (see Chapters 3 and 8).

It is preferable to cover the whole floor with the chosen type of hard flooring such as cork tiles or vinyl tiles. If only the border area is to be tiled, the tiled band must be wide enough to provide cover if the carpet or floorcovering piece should at some time in the future be turned through 90 degrees. The edge of border tiling under the carpet is likely to show through as a mark in your carpet at places of heavy foot traffic such as in front of the door; therefore it is always better to ensure that the main area of the room is at the same level as the border, i.e. it could be tiled all over, perhaps using a cheaper material for the central area which is always hidden by the carpet, or by insetting an underfelt which coincides in thickness with the border material.

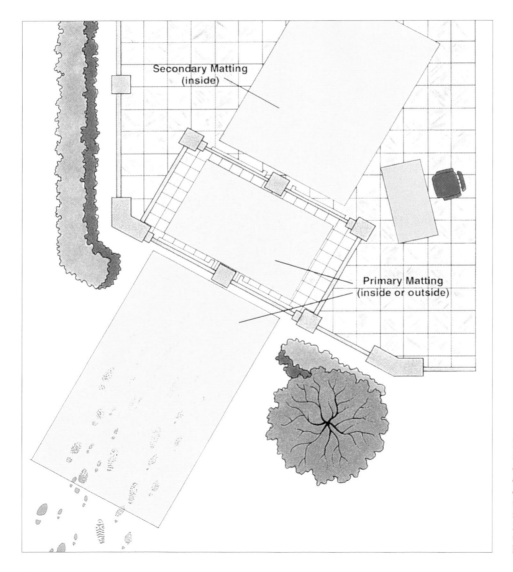

If you have a lot of young feet rushing in and out all day you might like to consider placing a mat outside the front door. Studies indicate that over 80% of dirt found in a house is brought in on the shoes. There should be at least 4 footsteps over the mats to be effective. 3M matting system has solved most of the problems, but remember you still have to clean the mat itself.

Chapter 6

INITIAL CARE
and ROUTINE CARE
of your Carpet

Should I vacuum-clean my new carpet?

A good quality vacuum cleaner is an essential part of equipment in every household. Daily cleaning is strongly recommended routine.

Yes. Do not believe the old wives' tale which claims that vacuuming a new carpet will harm it. Daily vacuuming of your new carpet is strongly recommended, and this routine should commence from the very moment that the carpet is laid.

Even though it is not noticeable, the household dust that settles on your furniture every day also lands on your carpet where it combines with the everyday dirt and grit walked in on our shoes. A build-up of soiling in your carpet can occur quite quickly, and can cause unnecessary and premature deterioration of the yarn affecting the good appearance of your carpet. Therefore regular vacuum-cleaning, right from the start, is important.

(See Appendix 2 which discusses in detail the choice and use of vacuum cleaners.)

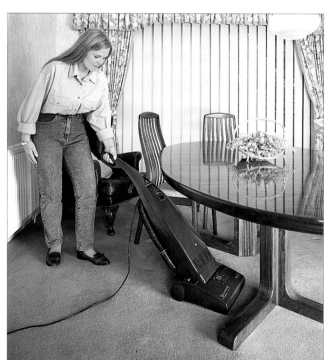

What is 'fluffing', and how should I deal with it?

You may be concerned to see fluff lying on the surface of your new carpet. This is called **fluffing** or 'shedding' and need not cause you concern. Fluffing appears because some loose fibres left in the pile after its final finishing at the factory, or short fibres in the yarn, work their way to the surface. The amount of fluffing that occurs with a typical new carpet represents only a tiny proportion of the weight of pile yarn.

Fluffing will tend to diminish in use and will not affect the life of the carpet at all. The only efficient way of removing this is by vacuum cleaning. If this is not done, or if an inferior type of cleaner is used, or one which is not properly maintained, the fluff will remain in the carpet and will be trodden back into the pile, resulting in a flat, matted and dull-looking carpet. It cannot be too strongly recommended that your new carpet should be regularly vacuum-cleaned fairly lightly, daily if possible, during the first two or three months after laying.

What is 'sprouting' and how should I deal with it?

You may find that the odd tuft or loop of the pile protrudes above the surface of your new carpet. This is called sprouting or shooting, and is usually the result of damage after laying, e.g. dragging something across the carpet, or perhaps a loop gets snagged by the claws of a domestic pet. **Never pull out a sprouting tuft or loop**. In cut-pile carpets, a protruding tuft can be cut off carefully with a pair of scissors to bring it to the same height as the surrounding pile. In the case of loop-pile woven carpets, snagged loops can usually be adjusted to their correct height by carefully raising an adjoining loop or loops with a knitting needle.

What is 'shading'?

All textile materials with a pile or nap will show some degree of shading, i.e. they will exhibit lighter or darker areas according to how the surface tufts or loops bend in relation to the direction of lighting on the carpet. Apparent lightening or shading occurs when the pile is brushed in different directions – a quite normal effect not only with most kinds of carpets, but also with velvet, suede, and even coconut-fibre matting. Such changes in appearance, or even footmarks, may be more apparent on carpets which have a lustrous pile.

The tufts throughout a new carpet will have a regular and uniform inclination, with each tuft in an almost vertical position. After a time, the tufts will gradually assume a greater slant in the areas of most use, and thus expose their sides to the light. As the sides of the tufts reflect more light than the tips, they will appear to be lighter in colour. There is no certainty that this will occur, but it seems to be a natural characteristic of all materials with a raised surface.

The effects of shading can be lessened if the pile is pulled back up by vacuum cleaner action, thus restoring the tufts or loops to their upright position and hence to much of their original colour. However, sometimes some degree of shading effect due to pile reversal becomes permanent, and the pile cannot be brushed back to its original angle, a condition called 'watermarking' or 'pooling' in which parts of the carpet appear to be darker or lighter when viewed from a particular direction. This effect may be more apparent in plain velvet carpets, in lightly patterned products, and in those having large unpatterned areas.

Shading will not affect the wear life of the carpet, and is likely be be less noticeable once your new carpet beds down in use. It is likely to be minimised or prevented if you follow the manufacturer's instructions to lightly vacuum-clean your new carpet frequently, and brush against the natural lay of the pile, which will lift the tufts upright and restore much of the original colour. Commence this care from the very moment the carpet is laid. With many modern carpets made of extremely durable synthetic materials, and those with wool/synthetic blends, it is virtually impossible to vacuum-clean your carpet too often!

I have some visible bands across my new carpet. Is this a fault?

This is probably not a fault in the carpet. Rolls of new carpet rest in racks in the manufacturers' or distributors' warehouses, with the result that parts of the carpet can be subject to sustained weight pressure on one section of the roll. This sometimes results in carpets exhibiting **crush lines** when they are first unrolled. The lines may be more noticeable in lighter, open-patterned carpets than in those which are darker or more heavily patterned. This is quite normal, and unavoidable, and should cause no concern, for the lines will disappear in a few weeks of normal use. Regular and thorough vacuum-cleaning will help them go quicker.

What can I do to prevent my carpet fading?

We can consider two kinds of fading; real fading due to the effect of light – and especially of direct light from the sun, and apparent fading due to flattening of the pile in the more frequently walked-on areas of your carpet.

If you have patio doors or large picture windows, the colour of your carpet might fade or change, especially if it receives direct summer sunshine. Woollen or wool-blend carpets naturally tend to react to sunlight, and this might affect their colour if they are subjected to prolonged sunshine. On the other hand, synthetic materials (such as nylon, polyamide, polypropylene and polyester) are able to achieve higher levels of colourfastness. Pastel shades of carpets are likely to be more vulnerable to fading than are the darker, richer colours. However, fading due to exposure to strong light can usually be prevented or minimised, and some form of protection at patios or picture windows is recommended, such as venetian blinds, curtains or roller blinds.

Even in carpets dyed strictly to British Standards, and although every care is taken in manufacture, natural textile materials cannot be dyed to be absolutely fast to light. Inevitably, the initial coloration will change with time and usage.

In the case of very light-coloured carpets, what looks like fading may simply be the optical effect of pile flattening in use (see the question on *Shading*, above), and perhaps some surface soiling. Regular vacuum-cleaning against the direction of the pile will help to lift the pile and will reduce or eliminate this apparent fading.

What are 'berber lines'?

Berber and tweed-effect (heather) carpets acquire their flecked look because natural yarns are randomly blended in their manufacture. As a result, there may be a line effect which might not have been visible in the carpet sample that you saw. The lines are a natural characteristic of the carpet, not a fault.

How can I minimise soiling and wear of my carpet?

◆ The most important thing is to regularly vacuum-clean your carpet as described above. See also Appendix 2.

◆ If you have good-sized and effective doormats at all the entrances to the house, dirt and dust carried on shoes will tend to be left on the doormat and not walked into the house.
　To be effective, the doormats must themselves be kept clean. Grit and dust can be removed from mats by shaking or beating, plus a thorough vacuum-cleaning. Some types of doormats, e.g. rubber-backed viscose/nylon pile mats, can easily be shampooed from time to time to remove all dirt and grit. Some types of doormats are suitable for washing in the washing machine – but carefully follow the maker's instructions. It is much easier to clean the doormats than to shampoo a soiled carpet!
　Sisal or coconut-fibre faced doormats tend to allow grit and dust to pass through them which will collect in the mat well. Mats of this type should ideally have a backing of rubber or pvc.

◆ In busy households where there is a lot of foot traffic in a hall or passageway, clear plastic runners or a linen drugget can be put down in wet weather to protect the carpet.

◆ The wear on the surface of your carpet can be accelerated by certain types of shoes which tend to grip the pile and can damage it. Rubber-soled shoes with strongly contoured soles, e.g. trainers which are designed for high grip, can ill-treat the pile, and can even pull out tufts, for example when turning around on one foot or when running up or down the stairs. It is recommended that only smooth-soled shoes are worn indoors.

◆ Placing castor-cups under the feet of heavy furniture will spread the weight over a greater area and minimise dents formed in the surface of the carpet.

◆ Rugs may be placed at strategic places to minimise wear, e.g. in front of the sofa and the fireplace.

◆ If the size and the shape of your room permit, you could rearrange the furniture from time to time to equalise wear over the surface of the carpet.

◆ If a loose-laid carpet is used instead of wall-to-wall carpeting, every year or two, perhaps during spring-cleaning, it could be turned through 90 degrees or 180 degrees to even the wear.

◆ If it is possible, shifting the stair carpets can compensate for the heavy wear that can occur, particularly at the nosings.

Note: Carpets are designed to be durable and will give years of good service under normal conditions of use and care. You will give your new carpet a good start if you follow the guidelines given in this chapter. It is unlikely that a carpet manufacturer would entertain any complaint relating to premature wear or 'pile pressure' if a carpet of lighter quality than is suitable for a given room is laid (see Chapter 4 regarding labelling of carpets to indicate their suitability for the various rooms in the house) or if the recommendations given in this chapter had not been fully carried out.

I have a tall piece of furniture which seems to be unstable on my new carpet. What should I do about it?

There is a risk that a tall piece of furniture – a shallow cupboard or a bookcase, say – placed on a thick carpet could be unstable and might topple forward. The danger may be greater if the piece of furniture has a flat base, so that the weight per unit area is insufficient to crush the pile down. Danger can be prevented by securing the piece to the wall by means of two or more stout 'mirror plates'. Stability can also be improved by placing four castor cups or small flat blocks of wood under the corners of the base.

Chapter 7

CLEANING *Your Carpet* and dealing with STAINS

1. CLEANING YOUR CARPET

How might one freshen-up a lightly soiled carpet?

If you wish to freshen-up a lightly soiled carpet, you should first vacuum-clean it thoroughly to remove surface dust. Before deciding to use a shampoo, see if your carpet responds to gentle treatment with a clean white absorbent cloth and warm water. It would be wise to test-clean a small out-of-view area first to check that the colours will not 'bleed' into each other.

1. Rub a small area of the carpet **lightly** with a clean white (not dyed) damp cloth, applying the moisture sparingly. Change the water frequently.

2. As you finish cleaning each small area, blot it thoroughly with a clean dry cloth.

3. Finish off each small area by lightly brushing the pile in its natural direction before moving on to the next section.

What should I do if the gentle water-only cleaning method is not successful for cleaning my grubby carpet?

Before deciding to use a proprietary carpet shampoo, you could consider using the services of a professional carpet cleaner. Loose carpets can be taken to the cleaners; wall-to-wall carpets and stair carpets can be cleaned in situ by the contractor.

If you decide to use a proprietary carpet shampoo, use a 'crystalising' shampoo, i.e. one which does not produce sticky residues, and follow the maker's instructions carefully. Do not be tempted to make up the shampoo mixture stronger than the maker's recommendations, for any residue of dried shampoo left in the carpet will lead to rapid resoiling. Again, it would be wise to test-clean a small out-of-view area first to check that the colours will not 'bleed'. Follow the procedure given in the previous answer. Carefully clean one small area of the carpet at a time, and then finish it off by lightly brushing the pile in its natural direction before moving on to the next section.

When is it necessary to wet-clean a carpet?

With use, all carpets become soiled, the degree of soiling depending on the amount of use and the circumstances. For example, the carpets in upstairs bedrooms, and those in an upper floor flat in which there are only one or two elderly occupants, will tend to keep clean longer than those in a house or ground-floor flat, and probably will only need wet-cleaning every three to four years. The carpets in a family home will tend to become soiled more quickly, so that ground-floor carpets may require wet-cleaning at intervals of eighteen months to two years. If wet-cleaning is delayed, it becomes more of a restoration process than a routine cleaning. Under all conditions of use, if vacuum-cleaning is carried out frequently and regularly as recommended in Chapter 6, soiling will be delayed.

Wet cleaning should always be carried out before the carpet becomes heavily soiled. However, if you should have the misfortune to have a spillage, your efforts to remove the stain may leave a patch which is noticeably cleaner than the surrounding area of carpet, and this may prompt you to wet-clean the whole carpet. (Refer to Appendix 2 regarding the Electrolux 'Electrojet' carpet cleaner.) If the carpet is only lightly soiled, before resorting to wet cleaning you may wish to consider other methods of cleaning it, e.g. absorbent cleaning powders and dry foam cleaners.

What is the function of absorbent cleaning powders?

Absorbent cleaning powders can be effective as a quick 'freshen-up' treatment or to help mask pet or other odours. Follow the maker's instructions carefully, and remove all traces of the powder by thoroughly vacuum-cleaning the carpet afterwards. If this is not done, soiling will soon occur again. After using your vacuum cleaner to remove the cleaning powder, replace the bag on your vacuum cleaner immediately.

Warning: Some people are sensitive to dusts and powders. Keep the windows open when using a powder treatment and when vacuum-cleaning the carpet.

When might one need to use a dry foam cleaner or carpet shampoo spray?

Products such as 'Vanish High Foam Shampoo' and 'Vanish Mousse' (both made by Benckiser Ltd) may be used with great care to deal with a grubby patch, and only after you have tested their effect on an out-of-sight part of the carpet. Carefully follow the manufacturers' instructions. After use, apply Method A which is described later. Remember that the newly cleaned patch may show up against any general slight grubbiness of the whole carpet and necessitate cleaning the whole carpet.

Could one use a carpet-shampooing machine?

For in-situ wet-cleaning of carpets, a '3-in-1' wet/dry vacuum cleaner may be used (see Appendix 2). Special shampoos are available for these, for example, 'Vanish High Foam Shampoo' made by Benckiser. Carpet shampooing machines may be hired from DIY stores or dry cleaners. If used strictly in accordance with the maker's instructions, they will successfully treat lightly soiled carpets. Such cleaners should not saturate the pile down to the base of the tufts, which means that the carpet will dry more quickly. Follow the manufacturer's instructions closely and note the advice in the following answer regarding too frequent use of these machines.

Are there any risks in wet-cleaning a carpet?

Yes, all types of carpets must be cleaned with great care for, if the dyes are not fast, some bleeding of the colours may occur. Also note that too frequent, or too harsh a chemical treatment, may remove any anti-staining agent with which the fibres of the pile have been treated, with the result that the carpet will soil more quickly after the treatment. A treated carpet, **if correctly cleaned**, should stand two or three wet-cleanings before reapplication of the anti-staining agent is necessary.

Too frequent wet cleaning of woollen or wool-blend carpets is not recommended. Indeed, the wet cleaning of heavily-soiled carpets of any type, and particularly of woollen or wool-blend carpets, is a task best left to professional cleaners. Wool is moisture-absorbent, and takes longer to dry than non-absorbent synthetic fibres. Remember that, unless a carpet has been specially made to be frequently wet-cleaned, inexpert treatment can lead to rapid loss of appearance and to disintegration of the backing materials of the carpet (with attendant odours!). Over-wetting can lead to shrinkage and to browning of the pile due to dye in the jute backing 'wicking' up into the pile.

If your carpet has become soiled or badly stained, you might make matters worse by trying to deal with it yourself. For example, you may 'fix' a stain permanently so that even a skilled professional will not be able to remove it. (See Appendix 3 for the address of the National Carpet Cleaners' Association.)

What must be done after the carpet has been wet-cleaned?

Whichever method of wet cleaning you use, open the windows and allow the pile to dry thoroughly before bringing the room back into use. It would be best not to replace any furniture until the carpet has dried completely; but, if it is necessary to replace furniture which has metal-tipped feet or metal castors, avoid rust-marks forming by slipping plastic or glass gliders (castor cups) under them. Similarly keep wooden furniture out of contact with the damp carpet, as the wood dye may stain the carpet. If you have no castor cups, use small pieces of polythene or folded plastic kitchen foil.

While your carpet is drying, it is important to maintain circulation of air. Open the windows. If possible, raise any low items of furniture so that air can circulate beneath and so prevent the formation of mildew or rotting of the carpet.

2. DEALING WITH STAINS ON CARPETS

Is a carpet with 'stain-resistant treatment' stain-proof?

No. While such treatments may enable a carpet to shrug off many contaminants, they do not make the carpet completely stain-proof. Such treatments cannot totally protect your carpet from stains caused by such contaminants as hot drinks or the vegetable dyes in some soft drinks. Wet-cleaning of the carpet may remove some of the treatment; even if the carpet is not wet-cleaned, the protective treatment will eventually be lost to some degree because of abrasion in ordinary use. However, carpets should retain a good degree of the protective treatment if they are cleaned correctly.

What are the First Aid rules for dealing with spillage on the carpet?

Apply the correct treatment as soon as possible to prevent a spillage causing a permanent stain. If in doubt what to do, perform the following 'First Aid' actions for all types of carpets except 'kitchen carpet':

◆ For fresh animal or baby accidents, and spillages of beer, wine, spirits, chocolate or fruit juices, immediately mop up as much as possible with a piece of absorbent white (not dyed) cloth, white blotting paper, unprinted tissue or plain kitchen-roll paper. Act quickly to remove as much of the substance as possible before it penetrates the pile of the carpet. A useful tool for such emergencies as spilt drinks would be a 'Wet and Dry' rechargeable hand-held vacuum cleaner (see Appendix 2).

◆ Speedy action is particularly important for spillages of emulsion paint or gloss paint, which must not be allowed to dry. Mop up as much as possible without delay, and then apply the treatment given in the table as soon as possible.

◆ Use a spoon or the back of a knife-blade to remove semisolids and greasy substances.

◆ To avoid damage to the texture of the yarn, do not rub too vigorously when treating a stain. To avoid spreading the stain, work from the edge of the stain inwards.

In many cases, where quick action has been taken, little penetration will have occurred, and all that is necessary is to give a final wipe with a clean damp cloth, leaving the pile sloping correctly.

How should I deal with spillages on 'kitchen carpet'?

For 'kitchen carpet' (short pile, all-synthetic fibre flocked carpet with a water resistant backing), follow this simple procedure:

1. Using a spatula or a blunt-edged knife or scraper, scrape up the stain or spillage straight away.

2. Scrub the stained area with a hard-bristled brush using a very weak solution of carpet cleaner solution (one teaspoonful of carpet cleaner to 5 litres (9 pints) of water).

3. Rinse the stained area thoroughly to remove all traces of the carpet cleaner solution. Scrape as much excess water as you can into a cloth.

4. Leave the carpet to dry.

5. Vacuum clean the carpet regularly as you would any other carpet. Set the brushes to the low setting so as to brush any dirt or fluff out of the pile.

How should I deal with small burns on my carpet?

Burns on a carpet containing man-made fibre due to a dropped cigarette or lighted match may result in unsightly damage which will be difficult if not impossible to remedy.

Pure wool carpets are more resistant to burns, and this helps to minimise the problem. If the pile is scorched, rub the area gently with sandpaper or the blunt edge of a table knife to remove the scorched fibre tips.

How should I deal with a serious wetting of my carpet – a burst pipe, say?

How badly your carpet is affected will depend on its construction and its quality. If the colours are not fast, some bleeding of colour may occur. Pure wool carpets and carpets with a high wool content are likely to absorb more moisture than carpets made of synthetic materials. How well your carpet stands up to severe wetting will depend largely on the nature of its backing. If the backing is absorbent, it will be more difficult to get it dried out.

In most cases, it will be necessary to take up the carpet so that it can be dried. Taking up the carpet also enables the floor to be dried. In the case of suspended floors where water has penetrated and perhaps damaged the ceiling below, the services of a builder may be required to take up floorboards and bring in a hot-air blower to dry out the joists and the undersides of the floorboards. Such blowers (which produce very hot air) should not be used to dry a carpet, but it may be possible to extract some of the water from the carpet by use of a '3-in-1' carpet shampooing machine (see Appendix 2).

Hanging a large carpet on a washing line is impractical because of the weight. In general it will be better if the carpet is kept flat, or at least not folded so sharply that the backing becomes distorted. **In these cases, as a matter of great urgency, it would be advisable to seek the services of a carpet professional** who can take the carpet to a warehouse or other place where it can be gently dried and kept flat during the drying process.

If urgent steps as described above are not taken to prevent damage to the carpet, it might be difficult to persuade your insurers to pay compensation to replace it. In any case, after a severe wetting, it is most probable that you will have to replace the underlay. Do not attempt to have the carpet re-laid until you are quite certain that the floor and the joists under it are completely dry.

There are three main methods recommended for dealing with stains, which are described here as Methods A, B and C. Refer to the following table which shows which method or methods are best for particular stains.

METHOD A

1. Blot with clean, white absorbent material to remove any excess liquid.

2. Gently sponge the stained area with either (a) a solution made of one teaspoonful of detergent for washing woollens to half a pint of warm water, or (b) a solution of proprietary carpet shampoo in warm water diluted to the manufacturer's instructions.

3. Rinse with clean, warm water.

4. Blot the damp patch thoroughly.

5. Gently brush the pile to its natural direction.

6. Make a pad of say five layers of white absorbent kitchenroll, and place on the damp patch. Place a heavy object– say a telephone directory – on top, and allow the patch to dry. (A damp carpet always dries from the surface. The absorbent pad will soak up any residual stain drawn to the surface during drying.)

METHOD B

Sponge the stain with a household dry-cleaning fluid in accordance with the maker's instructions. **Do not soak**. Refer to *warning* below.

METHOD C

1. Sponge the stain with a solution of one part of white vinegar to three parts of clean, warm water.

2. Leave for 15 minutes.

3. Sponge with clean warm water.

4. Blot the damp patch thoroughly.

5. Gently brush the pile to its natural direction.

6. Make a pad of say five layers of white absorbent kitchen roll, and place on the damp patch. Place a heavy object – say a telephone directory – on top, and allow the patch to dry.

TYPES OF STAIN

Alcohol (including dried stains) – Method C.
Animal and baby accidents – Method A.

Ballpoint pen – Sponge with methylated spirits (*), followed by Method A.
Beers, wines and spirits – Method A.
Bleach – Method A.
Blood – Method A.
Butter – Method B (*), followed by Method A.

Chewing gum – Apply a freezing agent and break gum away when hard, followed by Method B (*).
Chocolate – Scrape off excess, followed by Method A.
Cola (soft drinks) – Method A.
Cooking oil – Method B (*) followed by Method A..
Cosmetics and lipstick – Method B (*); if unsuccessful, try Method A.
Cream – Method B (*) followed by Method A.

Egg – Method A.

Floor wax – Method B (*).
Fruit juice – Method C, followed by Method A.
Furniture polish, shoe polish – Method B (*), followed by Method A.

Gravy and sauces – Method B (*), followed by Method A.
Grease and oil – Method B (*), followed by Method A.

Ink (fountain pen) – Method A.

Mineral water, tonic water – Method A.
Milk – Method A.
Mustard – Method A.
Metal polish – Method B (*), followed by Method A.

Nail polish – Dab with nail polish remover (*), followed by Method B (*) and Method A. (Note: Over soaking with nailpolish remover or similar solvents could damage carpet backings and some fibres. *Test first* on an out of sight patch.)

Paint (emulsion) – Blot off excess, then apply Method A.
Paint (oil based) – Dab with white spirit (*) or turpentine (*), followed by Method A (*).

Rust – Method B (*), followed by Method A. (Professional help may be required.)

Salad dressing – Method B, followed by Method A (*).
Soot – Vacuum-clean thoroughly, followed by Method A.

Tar – Method B (*). If necessary, follow by dabbing with eucalyptus oil (*).
Tea or coffee – Method A.
Tomato juice – Method A.

Urine (dry stain) – Method C, then sponge with cold water, followed by Method A.
Urine (wet) – Sponge with cold water, then apply Method A.

Vomit (dry stain) – Method C.
Vomit (wet) – Method A.

Wax – Scrape off excess, iron at low temperature over brown paper, then apply Method B (*)

*(*) Refer to **Warning***

Warning:
The fumes from substances such as dry-cleaning fluid, methylated spirits and acetone (nail polish remover) are flammable and can be harmful to health if inhaled. Before using such substances, open the windows. After use, let the room air thoroughly. Do not smoke, or create any spark or flame, nor use any electrical appliance in the room until it is free of fumes. Apply solvents with great care, for over-application can damage carpet backings such as latex, rubber or foam.

If you are in any doubt, contact a professional carpet cleaner.

You could ask your carpet retailer to recommend someone, or could enquire of the National Carpet Cleaners Association (see Appendix 4).

Chapter 8

FITTING *and* CARE

of Floorings and Floorcoverings

What are suspended floors and solid floors?

The term **suspended floor** is used to denote a floor supported on joists which are usually of wood, and may be an upper floor or a ground floor. A suspended floor at ground floor level will have a cavity or a cellar under it. Suspended floors are commonly boarded, i.e. constructed of wooden floorboards laid on timber joists. A better quality floor will employ tongued-and-grooved boards which hold in better alignment than plain butted boards and, having no gaps, do not let draughts through. For saving in cost, the surface of a suspended floor may be constructed of heavy grade chipboard laid on timber joists.

The term **solid floor** refers to a concrete floor which may be at ground floor level or, as in the case of many modern buildings, an upper floor consisting of steel-reinforced concrete. Solid floors at ground floor level in some older houses may be made of brick or other traditional materials.

What can I do about my uneven boarded floor?

As discussed in Chapter 5, an uneven boarded floor could be very destructive to a carpet laid on it. A smooth flooring surface would permit the choice of carpet, or of a timber floorcovering (e.g. strip flooring, wood mosaic flooring or wood block flooring), or other types of 'hard' flooring such as linoleum, cork tiles, vinyl (sheet or tiles) etc. To make an uneven wooden floor suitable for laying carpet or other type of flooring your options are:

◆ If any floorboards are showing signs of damp, rot, woodworm etc, you should have some or all of them replaced, and have the joists checked for signs of deterioration at the same time.

◆ If the floor is generally in good condition, you could have any damaged boards replaced. All proud nailheads must be punched down below the surface of the floor boards. Any boards with movement or bounce must be securely nailed or screwed to the joists. Any gaps between floorboards will need to be skillfully filled in with strips of wood, and planed level, or the boards taken up and re-laid. Finally, the surface may be smoothed by machine-sanding. Machine-sanding cannot be used to level an uneven floor which may require the attention of a joiner, for example, by overlaying the floor with plywood, chipboard etc.

Machine-sanding produces a great deal of dust, necessitating the operator to wear a dust-mask. The process is very noisy; so, if you live in a flat or semi-detached house, you might arrange for the work to be done at a time convenient to your neighbours.

◆ You could consider replacing the existing floorboards with hardwood tongued-and-grooved boards as discussed in Chapter 3. This would produce a durable and handsome floor which would enhance both the appearance and the value of your house.

◆ A less costly solution would be to have the existing floorboards covered over with composition board.

While considering your floors, find out wether it might be necessary to gain access to underfloor services of any kind. If so, you could make provision for this by installing hatches or lift-up sections of the flooring.

What should I do if woodworm, damp rot or dry rot is seen or suspected in the boards or joists?

You should get professional advice without delay. If the cause of the problem is damp, a new damp-proof course or other remedial building work may be needed. Timber treatment these days is carried out with chemical agents which are described as 'environmentally friendly', but they are still poisonous, and inhaling their fumes can be dangerous. After chemical treatment of the timber, the room should be left empty and the windows kept open for at least 24 hours before the room is occupied again.

Dealing with damp and rot in your floors should be given high priority. It would be regrettable if you went to the expense of laying new flooring or floorcovering, and then had to take it up to deal with damp or rot.

While work is being done on my suspended floor, could some insulation be added?

Yes. This is a good idea if the floorboards are going to be taken up anyway. Glassfibre insulation blanket can be laid between the joists supported on thin netting attached to the joists. It is also possible to use a type of rigid foamed lightweight insulating material which is cut to fit between the joists and is supported in this way, but ensure that only a fire-resisting grade is used. Note that both these types of insulation material are for reducing heat loss through the floor; they do not have any significant sound insulation qualities.

How should a boarded floor be covered with composition board or plywood?

If the joists are sound and a smooth level surface for the new carpet or flooring is desired, composition board (e.g. hardboard, plywood, fibreboard, chipboard, particle board etc) can be laid over the existing floorboards. Plywood sheets 6mm (1/4 inch) thick can be used for this; composition board is normally required to be at least 1/2 inch (12mm) thick. Firstly, the existing floorboards must be nailed down tight to the joists so that they do not bounce or squeak, and then the plywood or composition board is laid on to the floorboards and fixed down rigidly by countersunk screws. At the door openings, the bottoms of the architraves should be sawn off to permit the plywood or composition board to fit neatly under them.

If the floorboards are in bad condition, would it be possible to take them up and re-floor the room with chipboard?

Yes, this could be a practical solution and probably would be cheaper than fitting new floorboards. When the old boards are taken up, get an expert to check the beams for signs of damp, rot and woodworm before the new floor is installed.

If using chipboard (particle board), this must be of flooring grade which is made in thicknesses of 19mm (3/4 inch) and 22mm (7/8 inch). The thicker grade is generally preferred, but the 19mm thickness may only be used for floors in which the joists are spaced at less than 450mm (18 inches) apart. Tongued-and-grooved chipboard sheets are to be preferred as they prevent draughts at the joins. The sheets must be fixed to the joists with countersunk screws.

What kinds of flooring can be laid on the prepared surface of a suspended floor?

Given the basis of a firm, smooth floor surface, you would have the choice of laying carpet or selecting one of the range of 'hard flooring' materials, e.g. cork tiles, vinyl or cushion vinyl sheet, vinyl tiles, linoleum tiles, laid linoleum sheet, timber flooring etc. In rooms such as the bathroom, wc, shower room etc, as well as kitchens, pantries and utility rooms you could consider laying ceramic tiles or quarry tiles. (See the advice in Chapter 3 regarding the use of tiles on suspended floors and the laying of tiled floors in wet situations.)

(Right) Making a stylish entrance. Nothing is in better taste than this floor to a Yorkshire house. Vacheron stone, slightly sanded and honed, is provided by Stone Age.

Vinyl flooring required a firm smooth background to be really effective. This example of Nairn's Cushionflor and attractive geometric design, suggesting but not imitating tiling, provides a perfect surface for a dining corner in a kitchen and would also work well in a children's playroom.

Would it be a good idea to seal the surface of unglazed ceramic tiles or quarry tiles with linseed oil, a permanent sealing composition or a polish?

No. This is not recommended. Such substances are not absorbed into the surface of the tiles, and may make the tiles slippery and difficult to clean. The sealing agent can also permanently discolour the grout between the tiles in an unattractive way.

How should I routinely clean ceramic floor tiles and quarry tiles?

Routine cleaning consists of simply sweeping the surface with a clean soft broom or brush and, when required, washing the tiles with warm water to which a little ordinary household detergent has been added. (Washing tiles with soap is not recommended as this may leave a slippery scum, especially in a hard-water area.) The type of detergent recommended by the tile makers is described as 'neutral or nearly neutral, low sulphate detergent'; some well-known detergents of this type are 'Fairy Liquid', 'Gunk', 'Nu-Kleen', 'Stergene', and 'Sunlight Washing-Up Liquid'. Whichever cleaning aid is used, follow the maker's instructions. The usual method is to apply the dilute detergent solution to the floor, and – if possible – leave the floor wet for 5 to 15 minutes to allow the detergent to work. Then rinse the floor with clean water, remembering that it is the rinsing that removes the dirt.

In a kitchen which is floored with ceramic tiles or quarry tiles, how could one deal with ugly marks where something fatty has been spilt on the tiles?

The occasional very careful use of an abrasive cleaner might be beneficial in the case of unglazed tiles, but such cleaners should not be used on glazed tiles.

Greasy deposits and stains are best removed from both glazed or unglazed tiles by the use of a detergent containing an organic solvent, or by a **highly alkaline detergent**. Examples of these are: 'Taski Oil and Grease Remover' (made by Lever Industrial), and 'Quarryclean' (made by Dennis Ruabon Ltd). Follow the manufacturer's instructions carefully, and rinse the floor thoroughly after use.

How can one deal with non-fatty stains on unglazed floor tiles and quarry tiles?

Your first attempt should be to scrub the stained area carefully with an abrasive soap such as 'Gumption', 'Vim', 'Jif' or 'Ajax'. Persistent stains from certain inks, as well as bloodstains and coffee-stains, may be removed with household bleach, but this should not be used regularly. Some stubborn stains may yield to cleaning with scouring powder, or by the careful use of the pumice block. After dealing with the stain, thoroughly rinse the floor. Do not use steel wool, for particles of metal may be deposited in the grouting and form rust marks. If all your efforts to remove a stain fail, you could try asking the advice of the British Ceramic Tile Council (see Appendix 4).

Can I safely use a scrubbing machine on my unglazed tiled floor?

Yes, but only if it is a domestic-pattern machine fitted with brushes which give a light scrubbing action, and if the speed of the brushes does not exceed 450 revolutions per minute. (The use of a high-speed industrial-pattern scrubber could damage your tiles.) Follow the manufacturer's instructions, and remember that it is the rinsing that removes the dirt. The use of a scrubbing machine on glazed tiles is not recommended.

Are vinyl floorcoverings easy to lay?

Vinyls come in a range of widths that will permit jointless fitting in most room situations. This type of floorcovering can be 'loose laid', that is, the edges which might be kicked up at joints and doorways should be fixed with an approved adhesive over a width of 8 to 10cm. However, it is generally better for the material to be stuck down all over – and this is essential if domestic appliances are likely to be moved about over its surface. Joints can be sealed with the use of an approved 'cold weld' adhesive. When purchasing patterned vinyls, remember to purchase a sufficient amount to allow for pattern matching. To avoid shade variation within an installation, always purchase material having the same colour batch number, and reverse-lay the lengths (if the pattern permits).

Vinyls are available in plain coloured strips, squares and tiles of various sizes, so that patterns and designs that exactly fit the room can be achieved.

Vinyl can be successfully laid over floors consisting of wooden boarding, composition boards etc, and on to hard floors having an even surface; vinyl floorcoverings should not be laid on to an existing woodblock floor, nor laid over an existing vinyl product. The floor must be smooth, free from grit and wood treatment chemicals. It may be necessary to cover an uneven floor with composition board before applying the vinyl, otherwise the vinyl may deform and reveal the uneven supporting surface over a period of time, especially if the vinyl product has a glossy surface. Vinyl floorcoverings of any kind must not be laid on subfloors which are damp or prone to dampness.

How should one care for vinyl floorcovering?

Treated with ordinary care, good quality vinyl may be expected to last many years. Reputable manufacturers give a five-year guarantee on this material.

Damage can be caused to vinyl floorcoverings by cigarette burns and by sharp objects such as knives or heavy objects being dropped on them. They may suffer damage if a hot object is placed on their surface. To avoid scuffing the surface, do not drag any furniture or heavy objects across the floor without placing some protective material under them. To minimise staining, and to avoid the risk of someone slipping, any spillage or deposits on the flooring should be mopped up as soon as possible.

Routine care of vinyl consists of sweeping the floor thoroughly, ensuring that all grit is removed. Washing should be done with a small amount of detergent-based liquid cleaner in warm water – follow any instruction given by the manufacturers. After washing, rinse the floor well until all traces of the detergent have been removed – remembering that it is the rinsing that actually removes the dirt. Do not use solvent-based cleaners on vinyl, nor bleach, powder-based or liquid-based abrasives, nor strongly alkaline detergents (e.g. industrial cleaning fluids). Remember that vinyl flooring is slippery when wet.

As an aid to keeping the vinyl flooring clean, place doormats at the entrances to reduce the amount of dirt and gritty particles walked into the house. Caution: Do not place latex-backed or rubber-backed mats on the vinyl – they may cause discolouration.

How does one deal with a rug that tends to curl up?

A practical hint concerns lightweight rugs which have a coarse woven backing. These may tend to curl up and can cause someone to trip. You may be able to get rid of the curl by applying steam from a kettle spout to the backing and gently rolling the carpet in the direction opposite to the curl. Keep it in this position for some hours before releasing.

How can one prevent a rug from slipping on a smooth floor?

This problem may be solved by placing a strip of Dycem 'Slip Not' material or other proprietary high-friction material under each end of the rug.

When renovating my flooring, what should I do about the skirting boards?

No matter what kind of flooring you have, the skirting board is always of importance. A well-fitted skirting neatly defines the edge of your floor, and gives a finished look to the room.

Importantly, in rooms with suspended floors, a well-fitting skirting prevents the entry of draughts. Just consider: in a room of say, 12-ft by 12-ft, the total length of the skirting board would be 48-ft. Now, if there was a gap of just one-eighth of an inch all along it, the total area of gap would be 72 square inches – equivalent to an open hole in your wall of 8 or 9 inches square! Clearly, a snugly fitted skirting board will make your room feel warmer in winter, and will save you a great deal on your heating bill; so, if there is an unsightly and draughty gap under the skirting boards,

Some vinyl manufacturers provide a matching skirting to complement their floor tiles. Useful if yours is a new house and the usual timber skirting has not yet been put in. (Gerflor Ltd.)

it would be best to remove the skirting boards and re-fit them correctly.

When laying carpet on to a boarded floor, if the thickness of the carpet (including the gripper strips) is insufficient to completely close off the gap under the skirting boards, it will be best to remove the skirting boards and refit them closer to the floorboards. The gripper strip to hold the carpeting should be positioned as close as possible to the skirting boards.

As previously described, when laying carpet on wooden boarded floors, a layer of paper should be placed under the carpet to prevent soiling from draughts coming up between the boards.

If renovating an older house, replacing the skirting boarding with one of modern design will help to create a contemporary appearance. In some older houses, the high Victorian skirting boards have been removed; so, if you are creating or re-creating a period style room, it would be worth having high skirting boards of traditional design installed.

Skirting boards are usually painted the same colour as the window frames and other woodwork in the room; however, if you are striving to produce a certain design effect or using a special combination of colours as we discussed in Chapter 1, there is no law that says you should not paint your skirting board any colour that takes your fancy!

Could I use my old carpet as an underlay for my new carpet?

No. Never lay carpet on carpet. Every carpet should be laid on an underlay (underfelt) which will provide extra softness and heat insulation, and will extend the life of your carpet.

APPENDIX 1

Applied Arts (A catalogue of flooring products) available from Fired Earth plc, price £2.00.

Floors and Tiles by David Holloway and Fred Milson, ISBN 1853283801, Published by Charles Letts & Co Ltd.

Floor Style by Yvonne Rees; ISBN 0747201196, Published by Headline.

Guide to Contract Flooring Published by Contract Flooring Association.

The Home Expert by D G Hessayon; ISBN 09035052X, Published by PBI Publications.

Installation Manual for Textile Floorcoverings Published by the Contract Flooring Association.

Lighting Your Home by Renate Beigel and Stanley Lyons; ISBN 1870948947, Published by Quiller Press Ltd.

Oriental Carpets by Charles Ellis; ISBN 0906969816, Published by A.C.Black Ltd.

Reader's Digest New D-I-Y Manual ISBN 0276404564, Consultant editors: Nicholas J Frewing and Tony Wilkins. Published by The Reader's Digest Association Ltd. 1st Edn 1987, reprinted with amendments 1989.

Les Sols by Jane Scott; ISBN 2700053125, Published by Librairie Grund (in French).

APPENDIX 2

VACUUM CLEANERS

VACUUM CLEANERS

(The following information on vacuum cleaners has been provided by Electrolux)

What sort of vacuum-cleaner should I use?

◆ **For cut-pile or cut-loop-pile woven carpets.** Ideally, the vacuum cleaner employed should be an upright model with a rotary brush action. The brush action helps to raise the pile as well as brushing out and removing dust which settles from the air, and the dirt which is carried in on shoes.

◆ **For loop-pile tufted carpets including shag-pile and extra-long pile carpets.** A suction-only vacuum cleaner is recommended, for example, a cylinder cleaner or the use of the separate cleaning head connected to an upright cleaner. (The pile of shag pile and extra-long pile carpets may also need to be raised with a special rake – see Chapter 2.) If a rotary brush action vacuum cleaner were to be employed on a loop-pile tufted carpet over a long period, one might end up with an effect similar to 'brushed nylon' on the surface of the carpet. However, the use of a vacuum cleaner with adjustable brush height will enable this effect to be minimised or avoided entirely.

Is a vacuum cleaner with a beater-bar recommended?

No. The traditional approach to carpet cleaning was to use a vacuum cleaner with a beater-bar to agitate the carpet, and to lift the dirt by means of suction, the airflow passing through the fan into the dustbag. Because the continuous use of a beater-bar cleaner tends to accelerate the wear on the carpet, a vacuum cleaner of modern design, such as one providing extra suction power and a brushroll, is to be preferred.

What types of vacuum-cleaners are available?

The range of choice is extensive; for example, the products in the Electrolux range include the following:

◆ **Upright vacuum cleaners with a brush roll.** Upright vacuum cleaners are usually chosen for households which have extensive carpeting. Electrolux upright cleaners

An upright vacuum cleaner with a rotary brush action is the ideal tool for the care of cut-pile and cut-loop-pile woven carpets. The brush action helps to raise the pile. Vacuum cleaners in the Electrolux 'Contour' range have a kit of accessories including extension rods and flexible hose to give an 8-foot reach, enabling effective cleaning of curtains and furnishings as well as floors and stairs. (Electrolux Ltd.)

range from a lightweight 600-watt model having separate tools, to sophisticated cleaners having many useful technical features and controls, with motor ratings up to 1000-watts and having their tools 'on board'. The top of this range of upright cleaners, the 'Airstream 2', has a 1000-watt motor, on-board tools, a multi-stretch hose which permits a whole flight of stairs to be cleaned without moving the cleaner, a unique high-filtration dustbag, and an electrostatic filter which retains 99.99% of the dust picked up.

◆ **Cylinder vacuum cleaners.** These remain popular in homes where there are a variety of surfaces or awkward stairways and confined spaces to be cleaned. Electrolux has carried out research and development to find the best way of obtaining the right combination of high suction and airflow, and have created their twin-fan microbalanced motor unit. The result is a range of cylinder cleaners with increased durability and reduced noise. Electrolux cylinder cleaners range from lightweight models up to their 'Excellio' range having 1350-watt high-suction, with high filtration efficiency and low noise levels (70 decibels)

◆ **3-in-1 vacuum cleaners.** These are of value in any size of home where it is desired not only to vacuum-clean but also to be able to shampoo carpets. 3-in-1 cleaners combine the functions of dry pickup, wet pickup and shampooing action. The Electrolux 'Electrojet 1400-watt' cleaner has a totally integrated shampoo tubing system, a 4-litre easily removable shampoo tank, a unique 10-inch jet spray system, a squeegee for hard floors, an upholstery nozzle for cleaning and shampooing furniture, and a full set of 'dry' accessories.

The Electrolux 'Electrojet' is a 3-in-1 vacuum cleaner with the capability both of vacuum-cleaning and shampooing carpets. (Electrolux Ltd.)

The Electrolux 'Airstream 2' upright vacuum cleaner has a kit of on-board tools including a multi-stretch hose which permits a whole flight of stairs to be cleaned without moving the cleaner. (Electrolux Ltd.)

◆ **Hand-held vacuum cleaners.** These are useful for small cleaning jobs when it is not necessary to get out the main cleaner. The Electrolux 'Liberator' range includes small but powerful rechargeable models for cleaning carpets and upholstery, and in the car. The 'Wet and Dry' model is invaluable for picking up wet spills from a carpet as well as dry debris. The 'Tempest' model has a 300-watt motor, a rotating brush roll, and a 7.5m flex, making it ideal for stair cleaning and upholstery.

The Electrolux 'Tempest' hand-held vacuum cleaner, with its 300-watt motor, has a rotating brush-roll and 7.5m of flex, making it ideal for stair cleaning and care of upholstery. (Electrolux Ltd.)

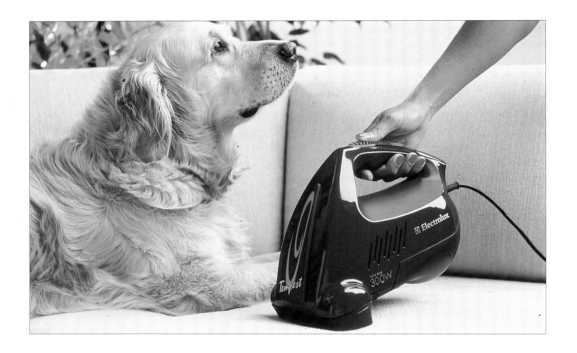

How does a vacuum cleaner with the extra suction power work?

Vacuum cleaners in the Electrolux range of Extra Suction Power cleaners, have a construction which uses two lightweight high-speed fans instead of one heavy duty fan, resulting in machines of lower weight which give more suction power. The air which carries the dirt passes directly into the dustbag (not through the fan) and then through an air filtration system which traps the dust within the cleaner. The clean filtered air then travels out over the motor to cool it. This construction results in the machine having considerably greater suction power than earlier vacuum cleaners, thus making the accessories much more effective on upright models. Top of the upright range is their 'Airstream' vacuum cleaner which has a powerful 1000-watt twin-fan motor to suck the air and dirt directly into the unique 'substrate-blown microfibre' high-filtration dustbag and electrostatic filter which retains 99.99% of the dirt and dust picked up.

How should the vacuum cleaner be used?

If using an upright cleaner, check that it is adjusted correctly for the height of the carpet pile. Whatever type of vacuum cleaner you use, for maximum efficiency make sure that you start with an empty dustbag and change it regularly. Filters need to be changed at least twice a year. Your cleaner will do its job more effectively if you pass it over the carpet slowly, giving each part at least six good strokes. This will ensure that the carpet gets a thorough cleaning right down to the base of the tufts where it is most needed. The daily vacuum-cleaning of your home can also be an opportunity to air the rooms thoroughly, and thus help to alleviate distress to those people with respiratory problems; however, if your vacuum cleaner does not have a micro-filter to trap very small dust particles which are drawn out of the carpet, these will be blown back into the room and can cause distress to asthma sufferers.

(The following information has been approved by National Asthma Campaign)

What are the essential facts about house dust mites?

It is a normal function of human skin to shed microscopic scales. These scales form part of the dust found in the cleanest of homes. The house dust mite is a microscopic insect whose only diet is scales of human skin. The mites are probably present in every home and building occupied by mankind, and doubtless they existed for millions of years before the microscope enabled us to be aware of the presence of these minute scavengers. The mites themselves are harmless to man, but their incredibly small droppings are light enough to become readily airborne, and may be inhaled by humans and act as an allergen. It is only people who are sensitive to allergens, i.e. some sufferers from hay fever, eczema or asthma, who may have a bad reaction to airborne house dust mite faeces. Research continues into whether exposure to high levels of allergens in early infancy might cause asthma, but this is not yet proven.

If I were to clean my home with an advanced vacuum cleaner having a micropore fine filter, would this relieve my asthma or hay fever?

No, but it is believed that you would be less likely to suffer an asthmatic or hay fever attack due to the presence of airborne allergens while you were actually doing the vacuum-cleaning. A fine filter vacuum cleaner will certainly make your carpet cleaner, for if the filter is fine enough and no particles are blown out from the exhaust of the vacuum cleaner, the minute particles sucked out of the carpet will not be discharged into the air to settle on the carpet again. A vacuum cleaner with a micropore filter, such as the Electrolux 'Airstream 1000', is recommended as being likely to improve the hygiene of your home significantly.

If I had no carpets at all in my home, would this ease my asthmatic or hay fever condition?

If the sufferer is sensitive to house dust mites, this could be helpful, but only if in combination with other measures. House dust mites thrive in bedding and upholstery as well as in carpets. At any instant, the density of house dust mites on a plain tiled floor is probably a quarter of that in a deep pile carpet, but the numbers change significantly with every waft of air, so the air pollution at any instant might be far higher than if the allergens were lying harmlessly trapped in the pile of your carpet. If you are an asthma sufferer, even if you were to live in an environment having no soft furnishings at all which could harbour house dust mites, you could still suffer an attack if you are sensitive to other allergens in your home. Different people have different triggers; some are avoidable, such as smoking, contact with cats etc. You could be prone to an attack due to contact with the relevant allergens in any environment outside your home. Avoiding triggers where possible is as important as taking any prescribed medication. Advice may be obtained from your doctor, or from National Asthma Campaign, Providence House, Providence Place, London N1 0NT. Calls to the Asthma Helpline (0345 010203) are charged as local calls.

APPENDIX 3

C A R P E T   W I D T H S

British carpets are usually made in the following widths:

Metric sizes		Imperial sizes	
4.00m	13ft 1-1/2ins	15ft 0ins	4.57m
3.00m	9ft 10ins	12ft 0ins	3.66m
2.00m	6ft 6-3/4ins	9ft 0ins	2.74m
1.00m	3ft 3-1/4ins	6ft 0ins	1.83m
0.34m*	1ft 1-1/2ins	3ft 0ins	0.91m
		1ft 3-1/2ins*	0.39m

* Borders, woven two across

Widths are subject to manufacturing tolerance. BS 3655 specifies a tolerance of plus-or-minus 1.25%

APPENDIX 4

USEFUL NAMES AND ADDRESSES

1. TRADE ASSOCIATIONS

British Carpet Manufacturers' Association
5 Portland Place, London W1N 3AA
Tel: 0171 580 7155 Fax: 0171 580 4854

British Ceramic Tile Council
Federation House, Station Road, Stoke-on-Trent ST4 2RT
Tel: 01782 747147

Carpet Council Advisory Service
1 Chelsea Manor Gardens, London SW3 5PN
Tel: 0171 349 0773

Contract Flooring Association
4c St.Mary's Place, Lace Market, Nottingham NG1 1PH
Tel: 0115 9411126 Fax: 0115 9412238

National Association of Tile Distributors
39 Upper Elmers End Road, Beckenham, Kent BR3 3QY
Tel: 0181 663 0946 Fax: 0181 663 0949

National Carpet Cleaners Association
126 New Walk, De Montford Street, Leicester LE1 7JA
Tel: 0116 2543552 Fax: 0116 2854795

National Institute of Carpet Fitters
4d St.Mary's Place, Lace Market, Nottingham NG1 1PH
Tel: 0115 9583077 Fax: 0602 9412238

National Master Tile Fixers Association
39 Upper Elmers End Road, Beckenham, Kent BR3 3QY
Tel: 0181 663 0946 Fax: 0181 663 0949

2. MANUFACTURERS AND DISTRIBUTORS OF CARPET, TILES AND OTHER FLOORCOVERINGS

The companies marked * in the following selected list are members of the British Carpet Manufacturers' Association who manufacture domestic carpets. Companies marked # are distributors. The addresses given are for the head office or London showroom. The telephone numbers given are for customer enquiries. Catalogues may be obtained from your local retailer or agent, or directly from the companies, some of which will provide samples of their products.

Adam Carpets Ltd*
Greenhill Works, Birmingham Road, Kidderminster, Worcestershire DY10 2SH
Tel: 01562 822247 Fax:01562 751471
Plain tufted carpets (saxonies and twist pile), patterned tufted carpets; carpet tiles

Amtico
Kingfield Road, Coventry CV6 5PL
Tel: 1203 861400 Fax: 1203 861552
Vinyl floorcoverings

Armstrong World Industries
Floor sales office, Fleck Way, Teeside Industrial Estate, Thornby, Cleveland TS17 9JT
Tel: 01642 763224 Fax: 01642 750213
Vinyl tiles and flooring

Axminster Carpets Ltd*
Gamberlake, Axminster, Devon EX13 5PQ
Tel: 01297 33533 Fax: 01297 35241
Axminster carpets for all domestic installations

BMK Ltd*
9-10 Savile Row, London S1X 1AF
Tel: 0171 437 3828 Fax: 0171 287 9380
Axminster and Wilton carpets (plain and patterned), tufted carpets (plain and patterned)

Bonar & Flotex
High Holborn Road, Ripley, Derby DE5 9BR
Tel: 01733 744121 Fax: 01773 142
Flocked 'kitchen carpet' with water-resistant backing

Brintons Ltd*
21/23 Queensdale Place, Holland Park, London W11 4SQ
Tel: 0171 602 8662 Fax: 0171 603 2653
Custom design and stock ranges of 80% wool/20% nylon Axminster and Wilton carpets; carpet tiles

Brockway Carpets Ltd*
Hoobrook Works, Kidderminster,
Worcestershire DY10 1XW
Tel: 01562 824737 Fax: 01562 752010
Axminster and plain tufted (velvet and pile twist) carpets, patterned tufted carpets, bespoke axminster designs

Carpets International (UK) plc *
Toftshaw Lane, Bradford BD4 6QW
Tel: 01247 681881 Fax: 01247 685161
(includes CV Carpets, Wilton Royal, Kosset, Abingdon, John Crossley, Lancaster, Donaghadee)
Axminster and wilton carpets and tiles; plain tufted carpets (saxony, velvet, velour twist loop pile); patterned tufted berbers and heathers

Cavalier Carpets Ltd*
Thompson Street, Industrial Estate, Blackburn,
Lancashire BB2 1TX
Tel: 01254 55321 Fax: 01254 673686
Axminster and tufted carpets; carpet tiles

Crucial Trading Ltd #
77 Westbourne Park Road, London W2 5QH
Tel: 0171 221 9000 Fax: 0171 727 3634
Importers of floorcoverings, rugs and mats made from natural materials such as coir, jute, linen, seagrass, sisal and wool

Dennis Ruabon Ltd
Hafod Tileries, Ruabon, Wrexham, Clwyd LL14 6ET
Tel: 01978 843484 Fax:01978 843276
Unglazed quarry floor tiles; porcelain floor tiles; fixatives for tiling

DLW Flooring
Centurian Court, Milton Park, Abingdon, Oxon OX4 4RY
Tel: 01235 831296 Fax: 01235 861 016
Linoleum, contract PVC, cushioned vinyl, rubber floorings, contract and domestic parquet, carpet and carpet tiles, needlepunch

Duralay Ltd
Broadway, Haslingden, Rossendale, Lancs BB4 4LS
Tel: 01706 213131 Fax: 01706 224915
Carpet underlay

Fired Earth Tiles plc #
Twyford Mill, Oxford Road, Adderbury OX17 3HP
Tel: 01295 812088 Fax: 01295 810832
Ceramic tiles & tile fixing service; rugs and mats; floorcoverings of natural materials including rush, sisal, seagrass and coir

Firth Carpets Ltd*
The Business Design Centre, 52 Upper Street, Islington,
London N1 0QH
Tel: 0171 354 5402 Fax: 0171 704 0725
Axminster, wilton and tufted carpets; plain and patterned tufted carpet

Flokati Rug Co Ltd
Unit C, 11B Weir Road, Balham SW12 0LT
Tel: 0181 6752442
Fleece rugs from Greece

Forbo-Nairn Ltd
Den Road, Kirkaldy, Fife KY1 2SB
Tel: 01592 261111 Fax: 01592 205461
Vinyl Infoline: 01592 643777
Linoleum, carpet tiles, cushioned vinyl

Freudenberg
LP Lutterworth, Leicestershire LE17 4DU
Tel: 01455 553081 Fax: 01455 556529
Rubber floorcoverings and needlefelt carpeting

Gates Rubber Company,
The Tredaire Division, Edinburgh Road, Heathall, Dumfries,
Scotland DG1 1QA
Tel: 01387 253111 Fax: 01387 268937
Tredaire carpet underlay

Georgian Carpets Ltd
Clensmore Mills, Kidderminster, Worcestershire DY10 2LH
Tel: 01562 820800 Fax: 01562 748580
Plain tufted carpets (saxony, velvet, velour and twist pile

Gerflor Ltd
43 Crawford Street, London W 1H 2AP
Tel: 0171 723 6601   Fax: 0171 723 9557
Cushioned vinyl floorcoverings

Great Walsingham Gallery
Great Walsingham, Norfolk NR22 6DR
Tel: 01328 820900
Rag rugs

Goodacre Carpets Ltd
Castle Mills, Aynam Road, Kendal, Cumbria LA9 7DF
Tel: 01539 723601   Fax: 01539 732442
Spool Axminster carpets

James Halstead Ltd
PO Box 3, Radcliffe New Road, Whitefield, Manchester, M25 7NR
Tel: 0161 766 3781   Fax: 0161 767 1100
Vinyl tiles and floorcoverings

Heuga (Interface Europe Ltd)*
The Gate House, Gatehouse Way, Aylesbury,
Buckinghamshire HP19 3DL
Tel: 01296 393244
Tufted, fusion bonded and fibre bonded carpet tiles

H & R Johnson Tiles Ltd
Highgate Tile Works, Tunstall, Stoke on Trent, ST6 4JX
Tel: 01782 575575   Fax: 01782 577377
Glazed and unglazed ceramic tiles

Junckers Ltd
Wheaton Court Commercial Centre, Wheaton Road, Witham,
Essex CM8 3UJ
Tel: 01376 517512   Fax: 01376 514401
Natural wood floors

Kährs UK Ltd
Unit 1 Timberlaine Estate, Gravel Lane, Quarry Lane, Chichester,
West Sussex PO19 2FJ
Tel: 01243 778747   Fax: 01243 541237
Natural wood flooring, parquet

Kosset Carpets Ltd
Toftshaw Lane, Bradford, West Yorkshire BD4 6QW
Tel: 01274 681881   Fax: 01274 685161
*Axminster and tufted carpets, patterned tufted (prints),
plain tufted carpets*

Lyle Carpets Ltd*
Tollpark Road, Wardpark East, Cumbernauld G68 0LW
Tel: 01236 738211   Fax: 01236 735503
Plain tufted carpet; saxony, velour and twist pile

Hugh Mackay Carpets
Roman House, Wood Street, London EC2Y 5BU
Tel: 0171 606 8491   Fax: 0171 588 7867
*Axminsters, Wiltons, Brussels Wilton and tufted carpets; plain tufted
carpets (saxony, velvet, twist and loop pile); rugs*

Marley Building Materials
Ltd Station Road, Coleshill, Birmingham B46 1HP
Tel: 01675 462081   Fax: 01675 465445
Quarry tiles

Marley Floors Ltd
Dickley Lane, Lenham, Maidstone,
Kent ME17 2DE
Tel: 01622 854000   Fax: 01622 854219
*Vinyl tiles in reproductions of woods, marbles, stones and terrazzo
effects; sheet vinyls; ranges of cushioned, textured and solid peel-and-
stick vinyl tiles*

Madeira Needlepoint
Rua Visconde de Anadia 44, 9000 Funchal, Portugal

Nairn Cushionflor
(see Forbo-Nairn Ltd)

Northern Ireland Carpets Ltd*
Comber Road, Newtownards, Co.Down,
Northern Ireland BT23 4QR
Tel: 01247 813864   Fax: 01247 812952
*Plain, tonal and patterned tufted carpet; saxony, twist and cut-loop
styles*

Annette Nix
Unit 24, Spitalfield Market, Steward Street, London E1 6AL
Tel: 0171 3772900
Designer/weaver of carpets

Paris Ceramics Ltd #
583 Kings Road, London SW6 2EH
Tel: 0171 371 7778   Fax: 0171 371 8395
*Ceramic floor tiles including terracotta, limestone, and terrazzo;
handpainted tiles; importers of antique terracotta and stone floors*

Pilkington's Tiles Ltd
PO Box 4, Clifton Junction, Manchester M27 8LP
Tel: 0161 727 1133 Fax: 0161 727 1122
Glazed and unglazed ceramic floor tiles

Louis de Poortere
(part of Stoddard Carpets Ltd)

Daniel Platt Ltd
Brownhill Tileries, Tunstall, Stoke on Trent ST6 4NY
Tel: 01782 577187 Fax: 01782 577877
Unglazed ceramic tiles and quarry tiles

William Pownall & Sons Ltd*
Eider House, 40 Ellesmere Street,
Manchester M15 4JY
Tel: 0161 834 7965 Fax: 0161 833 0965
Plain tufted carpets (saxony, velvet twist pile); patterned tufted carpets (graphics)

Richards International* (incl Kingsmeade and Spence Bryson)
Caponacre Estate, Cannock, Ayrshire KA18 1SH
Tel: 01290 421511 Fax: 01290 424211
Plain and patterned tufted carpets including saxonies, velvets, velours, twists and cut-loop

Sanderson Carpets (Arthur Sanderson & Sons Ltd)*
6 Cavendish Square, London W1M 9HA
Tel: 0171 636 7800 Fax: 0171 580 7861
Plain and patterned (graphics) tufted carpets; broadloom and carpet tiles; bespoke carpets)

Shaw Carpets Ltd*
PO Box 4, Dearne Mills, Darton, Barnsley, S.Yorkshire S75 5NH
Tel: 01226 390390 Fax: 01226 390549
Plain, tonal, patterned (printed) tufted carpet; saxony, velvet velour, twist, cut-loop and loop-pile styles; rugs

Stoneage
19 Filmer Road, London SW6 7BU
Tel: 0171 3857954/5 Fax: 0171 3857956
Stone flooring

Robert Stephenson, Oriental Carpets
1 Elystan Street, Chelsea Green, London SW3 3NT
Tel/Fax: 0171 255 2343
Oriental carpets

Steeles Carpets Ltd
The Carpet Mill, Barford Road, Bloxham, Oxon OX15 4HA
Tel: 01295 720556 Fax: 01295 721743

Stockwell Carpets Limited
3rd Floor, 51/52 New Bond Street, London W1Y 0BY
Tel: 0171 629 0626 Fax: 0171 409 2969
Sculpted, bordered and copied antique carpets

Stoddard Carpets Ltd*
15-19 Cavendish Place, London W1M 9DL
Tel: 0171 636 2612 Fax: 0171 631 5340
Axminsters, Wiltons, tufted and fusion-bonded carpets; bespoke

Threshold Floorings Ltd
Vorda Works, Highworth, Swindon, Wilts SN6 7AJ
Tel: 01793 764301 Fax: 01793 765319
Floorcoverings in natural fibres (jute, sisal, coir); doormats

Timber Management Ltd
Woodland Centre, Whitesmith, Nr Lewes, East Sussex BN8 6JB
Tel: 01825 872025
Hardwood and softwood flooring

Tiles of Stow
Langston Priory Workshops, Station Road, Kingham,
Oxon OX7 6UP
Tel/Fax: 01608 658951
Terracotta and ceramic floors; hand-painted tiles individually designed and decorated; hand-pressed relief tiles

Tomkinsons Carpets Ltd (Tomkinsons PLC)*
PO Box 11, Duke Place, Kidderminster, Worcestershire DY10 2JR
Tel: 01562 820006 Fax: 01562 820030
Axminsters and patterned Wiltons; plain and patterned (graphics) tufted carpets (velvet, velour and twist-pile); stock widths and carpet tiles

Ulster Carpet Mills Ltd*
Castleisland Factory, Portadown, Craigavon, Northern Ireland BT62 1EE
Tel: 01762 333177 Fax: 01762 333142
Axminster and Wilton carpets

Victoria Carpets Ltd*
Green Street, Kidderminster, Worcestershire DY10 1HL
Tel: 01562 823400 Fax: 01562 822679
Gripper Axminster, Wilton and tufted carpets; patterned tufted (graphics); plain tufted carpets (saxony, velour and twist pile)

Waveney Applegrowers – information from Crucial Trading

Westco Floor Coverings Ltd
Penarth Road, Cardiff CF1 7YN
Tel: 01222 233926 Fax: 01222 383573
Cork flooring tiles

Wicanders (GB) Ltd
Star Road, Partridge Green, West Sussex RH1B 8RA
Tel: 01403 710001 Fax: 01403 710003
Cork flooring tiles; wood flooring

Wilton Royal Carpets Ltd* See Carpets International (UK) plc

Wools of New Zealand
Development Centre, Valley Drive, Ilkley, West Yorkshire LS29 8PB
Tel: 01943 603888 Fax: 01943 817083

George Woolliscroft & Son Ltd
Melville Street, Hanley, Stoke on Trent ST1 3ND
Tel: 01782 208082 Fax: 01782 202631
Glazed and unglazed ceramic tiles

3. MANUFACTURERS OF PRODUCTS RELATING TO CARPETS, FLOORINGS AND FLOORCOVERINGS

Benckiser Ltd
Electro House, Farnsby Street, Swindon, Wilts SN1 5AH
Tel: 01793 612422 Fax: 01793 611572
'Vanish' foam shampoos and cleaning Mousse for carpets

John Cotton (Colne) Ltd
Spring Gardens Mill, Colne, Lancashire BB8 8EL
Tel: 01282 863550 Fax: 01282 869796
Manufacturers of underfelts for carpets

Dycem Ltd
Ashley Hill Trading Estate, Bristol BS2 9XS
Tel: 0117 955 9921 Fax: 0117 954 1194
'Slip Not' high-friction plastic sheeting material

Electrolux Ltd
101 Oakley Road, Luton, Beds LU4 9QQ Customer Care Desk
Tel: 01582 585858 Fax: 01582 588867
Vacuum cleaners including micropore filter cleaners, 3-in-1 carpet shampooing and vacuum cleaning machines, floor polishers; after sales service

Gradus Ltd
Park Green, Macclesfield, Cheshire SK11 7NE
Tel: 01625 428922 Fax: 01625 433949
Flooring accessories

Lever Industrial
Lever House, 3 St James's Road, Kingston-upon-Thames KT1 2BB
Taski Oil and Grease Remover for tiles

Dennis Ruabon Ltd
Hafod Tileries, Ruabon, Wrexham, Clwyd LL14 6ET
Quarryclean tile cleaner

3M Ltd
3M House, PO Box 1, Market Place, Bracknell, Berkshire RG1JU
Tel: 01344 858000 Fax: 01344 858278
Commercial Care EBU

APPENDIX 5

G L O S S A R Y

Note: All brand-names shown with initial capital letters in this list are acknowledged as Trade Marks.

Acrilan – A brand of acrylic synthetic fibre used in carpetmaking.

Acrylic fibres – used in carpetmaking are marketed under trade names including Acrilan, Dolan, Dralon, Leacril and Velicren FR.

Anso – A brand of polyamide synthetic fibre used in carpetmaking.

Antron – A brand of polyamide synthetic fibre for carpets made by Du Pont.

Anti-soiling agent – A treatment which may be applied to the surface of a carpet to resist the penetration of soiling into the pile material. See Stain Resist.

Anti-static agent – A substance applied to, or a treatment incorporated into the pile of a carpet and/or its substrate to prevent the accumulation of an electrostatic charge. See Static electricity.

Antron, Antron Excel and Antron Ultra Plus – Brands of polyamide synthetic fibre material used in carpetmaking.

Asphalt – A paving material consisting of particles of sand, crushed stone or gravel, bound together with bitumen. The material may be laid hot or cold, and hardens by chemical action and the evaporation of oily solvents.

Astra – A brand of polypropylene synthetic fibre used in carpetmaking.

Backing (to a carpet) – Backing may be primary or secondary. Primary backing is woven or non-woven material (usually synthetic) into which the pile yarn of a carpet is stitched. Secondary backing is the finishing layer (of foam, hessian, polypropylene, latex or pvc) which is applied to the primary backing of tufted carpets to improve the appearance of the back and to improve the dimensional stability and insulation properties of the product.

Berber (or berber style) – carpets are described in Chapter 2.

Bitumen – A brownish-black oily mineral substance used in making asphalt and as waterproofing agent for roofs etc.

Bleeding – The loss of dye from coloured material in a carpet due to contact with a liquid which is a solvent to the dye, causing spread of the dye to adjacent areas of the carpet or into other materials in contact with it.

Body carpet – Plain or unbordered carpet manufactured in widths from 690mm to 1m, mainly used for seaming or otherwise joining edge-to-edge into larger areas.

Bonded – The term 'fibre bonded' describes a textile floorcovering material composed of entangled textile materials bonded together by a mechanical, physical or chemical process or a combination of these processes. 'Fusion bonded' describes a textile floorcovering in which the pile is secured to the primary backing by adhesion.

Broadloom – Carpet of 1.83m (2 yards) width or more.

Brick – Bricks are blocks of pressed clay which have been fired in a kiln. Standard size housebuilding bricks (9" x 4.5" x 3") are available in a range of colours and textures. Thinner (Flemish) bricks are still manufactured for use in decorative walling and for laying old-fashioned brick paths.

Brussels – A type of loop pile carpet woven on wilton looms. (See Woven).

Bulked continuous filament – Synthetic fibres (e.g. polyamide or polypropylene) extruded in long lengths and 'crinkled' before being spun into yarn. This is done to give added bulk to the material. See also Staple fibres

Carpet square – A piece of carpet, usually rectangular, at least 1.83m (2 yards) wide, and usually loose laid.

Carpet tiles – Pieces of carpet or other textile floorcovering material, square or rectangular, which are laid upon the structural floor. May be loose laid, or fixed with adhesive. Some carpet tiles come with an adhesive backing protected by a covering of treated paper which is peeled off when laying.

Carved pile – Carpets in which the yarn of the pile is sheared at different levels to make a design. May be used to emphasise motifs in patterned carpets. See Pile finishes.

Ceramic tiles – Flooring tiles of fired clay, glazed or unglazed thin square, rectangular or other shapes of clay which are kiln fired. Available in a wide range of colours. Are laid with an adhesive on a solid floor or path foundation, and may be laid in patterns. See Terracotta.

Cobbles – Blocks of stone, usually square or rectangular, which may be laid in patterns especially for outdoor paths and drives.

Cement – A natural or synthetic mineral material in powder form which hardens on mixing with water. Used for building construction and surfacing. Cement mixed with sand forms mortar; mixed with sand and ballast (stones) it forms concrete. See Portland Cement.

Charisma – A brand of polypropylene synthetic fibre used in carpetmaking.

Coir – Fibre obtained from the husks of coconuts, used in carpetmaking. Also used to make woven textile floorcoverings and doormats.

Composition boards – Term used in this book to designate boarding materials which may be laid upon uneven floors to create a smooth surface before fitting carpeting or other fibre floorcovering, or vinyl or cork floorcovering etc. Composition boards include plywood, fibreboard, chipboard etc.

Concrete – A building material comprising an aggregate of stones and sand, cement and water. After mixing, it forms a hard durable mass. The surface of concrete can be left rough or may be screeded. Cement and concrete surfaces tend to produce dust unless they are sealed chemically, or coated with a cement paint which gives a durable non-dusting surface with choice of colour. Flat screeded floors provide an excellent support for terrazzo, or for synthetic rubber or vinyl floorcovering etc. See Screed.

Cotton – The soft fibre material surrounding the seeds of the cotton plant is used in making carpets and other floorcoverings.

Danaklon – A brand of polypropylene synthetic fibre used in carpetmaking.

Decorwool – Trademark for carpets having a wool content which conform with the quality test standards of Wools of New Zealand.

Dolan – A brand of acrylic synthetic fibre used in carpetmaking.

Downspun – A brand of polypropylene synthetic fibre used in carpetmaking.

Dralon – A brand of acrylic synthetic fibre used in carpetmaking.

Drop match – Where two or more pieces of similar carpet to be seamed together need to be moved in relation to each other in order for the pattern to match across their widths. This may take some extra carpet length which should be allowed for in the estimate. See also Pattern match.

Duron – A brand of polypropylene synthetic fibre used in carpetmaking.

Enkastat – A brand of polyamide synthetic fibre used in carpetmaking.

Excel – A brand of polyamide synthetic fibre used in carpetmaking.

Fading – Loss of colour in carpet or other floorcovering material caused by the actinic effect of light or by contact with airborne or liquid contaminants. See Pile flattening.

Fibres – Fibres used in carpetmaking: see Man-made fibres (Synthetic fibres), and Natural fibres. See also Bonded.

Figured carpet – Patterned.

Flocked – A method of carpetmaking in which short chopped lengths of fibres are applied to an adhesive-coated backing material by electrostatic attraction.

Flotex – tm of Bonar & Flotex Ltd for waterproof kitchen carpet made by electrostatic flocking process.

Friezé – (also called 'Hard twist') In carpets, the yarn may be heated or chemically treated and tightly twisted in manufacture to give the pile extra resilience and resistance to crushing.

Granite – A hard-wearing stone flooring material unlikely to be used in ordinary homes because of its cost.

Grinning – A trade term for the backing of a carpet being visible through the pile yarn, a condition that is particularly noticeable in carpets of poor pile density.

Grout – (a) A thin mortar used in building work to fill cracks and crevices in masonry. (b) A product used for infilling between ceramic tiles. May be coloured. Waterproof grouts are also used.

Gymlene – A brand of polypropylene synthetic fibre used in carpetmaking.

Hard twist – See Friezé.

Heather – See Berber

Hessian – A coarse woven material made from jute fibres, used as a floorcovering and as a backing to some tufted carpets.

Heuga – A brand of carpet tiles from Interface Europe Ltd Jute A natural fibre obtained from certain Asian plants and used in carpetmaking. See Hessian.

Leacril – A brand of acrylic synthetic fibre used in carpetmaking.

Lilion – A brand of polyamide synthetic fibre used in carpetmaking.

Linoleum – A hard-wearing floorcovering made of ground cork with linseed oil, wood-flour and resins, cured at high temperature and attached to a jute or fibreglass backing. Modern linoleums are much improved compared with the early material which was invented in 1860 by Frederick Walton, being more durable and more flexible, soft underfoot and warm to touch. Currently making a comeback in new colours and favoured by modern interior designers. Linoleum may be attached with adhesive to a solid floor. May be polished with wax polish. Jute-backed linoleum may deteriorate if water gets under it, e.g. from washing.

Man-made – fibres used in carpetmaking include those made from natural viscose (cellulose).

Marble – A natural stone material formed by heat and violent earth movements, which is characterised by having attractive grain patterns which are revealed by smoothing and polishing the surface.

Matted – Term to describe condition of a pile carpet when the pile material has been so compressed that individual tufts cannot be seen. In areas of the carpet where pile shading has occurred, the edges of these areas may be defined by a matting or merging of the pile material as the pile tries to lie in both its normal position and a different position. See Raking. See Shading.

Meraklon – A brand of polypropylene synthetic fibre used in carpetmaking.

Marquesa – A brand of polypropylene synthetic fibre used in carpetmaking.

Mortar – A mixture of cement and sand.

Mosaic – Flooring made of small ceramic tiles embedded in a bed of cement. See Chapter 3.

Nap – A fibrous surface produced on a fabric or felt in which part of the fibre is raised above the basic structure (as in a fibre bonded carpet).

Natural fibres – Those used in carpetmaking include coir, cotton, jute, silk, sisal and wool.

Nora – Brand of Freudenberg LP for rubber flooring and needlefelt carpeting

Nylfranc – A brand of polyamide synthetic fibre used in carpetmaking.

Nylon – A synthetic fibre material used in carpetmaking.

Olefin – See Polypropylene.

Pattern match (also called self match) – Where one portion of a pattern is repeated in full across the width of a carpet. See also Drop match.

Pile bursts – When the yarn of the pile of a cut pile carpet untwists and the tip of the tuft bursts open, leading to deterioration in appearance. This condition may be caused by insufficient treatment in manufacture in 'setting' the yarn, or by too vigorous application in wet-cleaning or stain removal.

Pile finishes – The pile of a carpet may be uncut (looped), or there may be a mixture of cut and uncut (looped) areas to create a textured design. The pile may be 'sculptured' (carved) into a pattern by having some areas with different length of pile and/or omitting the pile in some areas. See Carved pile. See Friezé/hard twist. See Saxony. See Shag.

Pile flattening – Compression of the pile of a carpet so that the sides of the tufts are exposed. This may give an effect similar to fading. The effect can be reduced if extra care is taken when vacuum-cleaning the most frequently walked-upon areas.

Pilling – Small accumulations of fibres on the surface of a carpet which may develop during wear, particularly with loop-pile carpets. The 'pills' are usually composed of the same fibres as the fabric, and in synthetic fibre carpets they are usually well anchored. Pilling can also occur if other textile fibres become entangled with the carpet pile, e.g. from rugs, from cotton fibres such as from candlewick bedspreads or towels in contact with the carpet, or hair from moulting domestic pets.

Polyester – A type of synthetic fibre material used in carpetmaking including that marketed under the tradename Trevia.

Polyamide – A type of synthetic fibre material used in carpetmaking marketed under tradenames including Anso, Antron, Antron Excel, Antron Ultra Plus, Enkastat, Lilion, Nylfranc, Tactesse, Timbrelle, Zeftron and Zefstat.

Polypropylene – also known as Olefin. A type of synthetic fibre material used in carpetmaking marketed under tradenames including Astra, Charisma,

Danaklon, Downspun, Duron, Gymlene, Marquesa, Meraklon, Prismatique and Zylon.

Polyvinyl chloride (PVC) – See Vinyl

Portland Cement – Modern cement material formed by firing a slurry of clay and limestone and then grinding it to a fine powder, a process invented by Joseph Aspdin in 1824. So called because its colour is similar to Portland stone. Cement surfaced floors are abrasive to shoes etc unless sealed or painted with concrete paint.

Prismatique – A brand of polypropylene synthetic fibre used in carpetmaking.

PVC (Polyvinylchloride) – See Vinyl

Raffia (Raphia) – Fibre derived from the African raffia palm which is used for weaving mats.

Raking – Shag carpets need to be treated with a carpet rake to keep the pile from flattening.

Rubber flooring – Natural rubber flooring material, made from the latex from rubber trees, is durable and stable if 'vulcanised', i.e. treated with sulphur and heat in manufacture. However, in the UK natural rubber is no longer used for flooring. See Synthetic rubber flooring.

Saxony – Carpet with longer-than-average pile. See Pile finishes.

Screed – A smooth final surface skim of cement or cement and sand, applied to a floor.

Self match – See Pattern match

Shading – A change in the appearance of textile floorcoverings and pile carpets, due to differences in light reflection from localised alterations of the orientation of the tufts or loops. This is unrelated to the method of manufacture and is not a manufacturing fault. Shading is not detrimental to the durability of the carpet. Shading may be temporary i.e. reversible (see Raking), or permanent (known as 'watermarking' or 'pooling'). Shading may occur through 'tracking', i.e. localised compression of the pile due to repeated walking over the same part.

Shag – Carpet with pile greater than 15mm in height, but not densely tufted. Such carpets need to be raked to keep the pile from flattening. See Raking.

Silk – A fine lustrous natural fibre produced by the silkworm which is used in oriental carpetmaking.

Sisal – A stiff coarse natural fibre derived from the leaves of a Mexican plant which is used in the manufacture of some floorcoverings.

Slate – Widely used for roofing; also makes an excellent hard-wearing surface for floors if skillfully laid. Colour of slate varies with source, e.g. that from Spain ranging from grey to dark blue, grey-blue or purple slates from North Wales, green slate from the Lake District, and brown and red colour slates from Africa.

Stainmaster tm: Du Pont; – a brand of anti-staining treatment of polyamide synthetic fibre used in carpetmaking.

Stain Resist – Stain resistant treatments may be applied to carpets in manufacture to reduce the rate of absorption of staining substances such as fruit juices, beverages, foodstuffs etc.

Staple fibres – Synthetic or natural fibres made from predetermined short lengths spun into continuous lengths of yarn and used in carpetmaking. Also known as bulked continuous filament.

Static electricity – An electrical charge which can be generated in carpets subject to friction – even by shoes walking over them. The effect is greatest in very dry atmospheric conditions. See Anti-static.

Stone – Hard natural rock material which is used to face a structural floor. The appearance of stone materials when they are ground flat and polished may differ greatly from their appearance when rough-hewn. Stones used for flooring include granite, limestones of various colours, sandstone, and marble.

Suspended floor – A floor consisting of joists (usually of timber, but may be steel in modern buildings) which support the flooring material (usually wooden floorboards or composition board). This construction is commonly used for the upper floors of houses, and is also employed for ground-floor floors where there is a cavity or cellar under the floor.

Synthetic fibres – Those used in carpetmaking include Acrylic, Nylon or Polyamide, Polyester and Polypropylene materials. Man-made fibres include also those made from natural Viscose.

Synthetic rubber flooring – This material has completely replaced natural rubber for flooring in the UK, and is used widely. It is usually patterned with small raised studs to improve the anti-slip quality and give resilience underfoot. It has better resistance to cigarette burns than does vinyl. Available in many colours. The joins in large areas can be welded together to make the covering continuous. See Vinyl.

Tactesse – A brand of polyamide synthetic fibre used in carpetmaking.

Terracotta – Tiles formed from clay and kiln fired. The term is particularly applied to tiles of orange or red/brown colour which are unglazed.

Terrazzo – Consists of small coloured flat stones or fragments of marble etc, laid into a layer of cement and ground off flat. Large areas have to be fitted with expansion joints to prevent cracking. Costly, especially if the coloured stones are arranged in complex patterns or formed into artistic representations. The surface is easily cleaned and longlasting.

Tile – This term may apply to Ceramic, Cork or Carpet tiles.

Tolerance on dimensions of carpets – The British Standard tolerance is plus-or-minus 1.25 percent for width when carpet is cut from a roll. The same tolerance applies to both width and length of rugs and carpet squares, i.e. large rugs having a shortest dimension of 1.83m (2 yards). (See Appendix 5)

Timbrelle – A brand of polyamide synthetic fibre used in carpetmaking.

Trevira – A brand of polyester synthetic fibre used in carpetmaking.

Tuft density – The number of tufts per unit area of a carpet. The denser the pile, the less likely it is to flatten.

Tufted – Carpet in which the pile fibres are stitched into a preformed backing during manufacture.

Velicren – VR A brand of acrylic synthetic fibre material used in carpetmaking.

Velour – Carpet with a smooth velvet-like finish.

Venetian mosaic – See Terrazzo.

Vinyl – Term used to describe a range of flooring materials available in sheet or tile form, based on the plastic polymer material polyvinyl chloride (PVC). May be backed with PVC foam to increase resilience underfoot. Vinyl floorcoverings are available in an enormous range of surfaces which mimic wood blocks, ceramic tiles, marble – even bricks – and may be coloured and textured realistically. Vinyl floorcoverings are available in a range of qualities, depending on their chemical composition which determines the stability and wearing qualities of the material.

Viscose – Man-made fibres of natural viscose used in carpetmaking.

Wool – The dense soft natural fibre from the coats of sheep and other animals, used in carpetmaking.

Woven – This term describes carpets such as Axminster, Wilton and Brussels in which the backing is woven at the same time as the pile yarn is inserted. See Woven back.

Woven back – A term used to describe a jute secondary backing on tufted carpet. (Do not confuse this with the backing of Axminster or Wilton carpet which is woven at the same time as the pile is inserted.) See Woven.

Zefstat, Zeftron, Zylon – Brands of polyamide synthetic fibre material used in carpetmaking.